David Marks was appointed Professor of Hematology and Stem Cell Transplantation at the University of Bristol in 2007 and was previously director of the Bristol Bone Marrow Transplantation Unit in 2003. David brings both an outsider's perspective on the NHS as an Australian who spent his early life, including medical training, in Australia and later worked for three years in Philadelphia, and an insider's perspective as a distinguished professor firmly embedded in the medical establishment, having lived in the UK for over three decades. His clinical practice and research focus on stem cell transplantation and the treatment of acute lymphoblastic leukaemia (ALL). He is a world authority in cellular therapy for adult ALL but is also deeply interested in patient welfare, a major preoccupation of Life Blood. He has been a writer his whole professional life, but this is the first book he has written for a general, non-medical audience.

To three women: my mother, my wife Jenny and my daughter Zoe.

To my patients with leukaemia.

# David Marks

---

# LIFE BLOOD

## Stories of Leukaemia Patients and Their Doctor

**AUSTIN MACAULEY PUBLISHERS™**

LONDON ∗ CAMBRIDGE ∗ NEW YORK ∗ SHARJAH

A CIP catalogue record for this title is available from the British Library.

ISBN 9781035833689 (Paperback)
ISBN 9781035833702 (ePub e-book)
ISBN 9781035833696 (Audiobook)

www.austinmacauley.com

First Published 2024
Austin Macauley Publishers Ltd®
1 Canada Square
Canary Wharf
London
E14 5AA

First of all, I have to thank my mum for encouraging my reading and writing and for insisting that proper English was spoken in our house.

Alison Powell of WriteClub helped me learn the craft of writing and taught me a lot about plots and visual description. My fellow writers on the courses are too many to name, but they were endlessly positive but were also usefully critical. I also thank them for their camaraderie and for coming up with ideas for the book's title.

My daughter Zoe, who did an English degree at Durham and writes beautiful English, read parts of the book but also reminded me that she must have inherited her talents from somewhere.

I had a number of beta readers who gave up their time to read some quite early writing. Many of them belong to my wife's long-established book club. Special thanks to Ann Low and Julie Molesworth for their enthusiasm and erudite criticism.

Jess Farr-Cox, of The Filthy Comma, acted as far more than a proofreader. Punctuation, grammar, word choice and sequencing were some of the things she helped me with. Most of all, she really cared about my work because she thought it was worthwhile.

Adam Crowther of BBC Radio Bristol Upload allowed eleven excerpts from my book to be read on the radio and interviewed me five times from 2021 to 2023. He also believed in me, and this faith really helped.

To all the patients who allowed me to tell their stories, particularly those who allowed me to use their real names, thank you for your generosity and trust. Apart from helping and inspiring me, you will also help other patients with leukaemia and their families fight the good fight.

Several colleagues and friends told me not to give up: they were right! They are too many to name, but hopefully, they have bought a copy!

Some of the agents who read my submission rejected my book but made me feel that the project was worthwhile nonetheless: thanks.

To everybody at Austin Macauley, thank you for taking me on and bringing the book to its audience.

Finally, the biggest debt is due to my wife Jenny, an inveterate reader. Thanks for reading my stuff and for putting up with seemingly endless struggles to find an agent and publisher, and for keeping me going through some very dark days where I lacked self-belief.

# Table of Contents

# Author's Note

The great majority of the patients I write about gave written consent for me to tell their story unabridged, using their actual names. Almost none of them wanted to see what I wrote before approving it. This is a measure of their trust in me, and I thank them for being so generous in sharing their stories. Other patient journeys have been changed in small ways to disguise identities, and in some cases, the stories are composites of multiple patients, always with the intention of sticking closely to the medical truth. I have generally avoided using colleagues' names and have modified details and events to preserve anonymity.

# Introduction: Blood

Blood should be a reddish colour. Sometimes, when it is deprived of oxygen, it is a worrying dark blue, the colour of cyanosis. Very occasionally, in a patient with carbon monoxide poisoning, it is what we call cherry red. Blood affects a person's skin colour: this is key to our perception of whether they look well or not.

My first proper encounter with patients with serious blood diseases was in 1983, my second year as a junior doctor, when I was the sole medic on a three-month haematology rotation. Even before this rotation, I knew haematology would be my chosen path. Haematology patients have serious illnesses, but they are treatable, and the interaction with science is never far away. Normally, there would be a haematology registrar, a more senior doctor who reported to the consultants, but this registrar had a long-term illness, so I was left on my own to run the ward on a day-to-day basis.

In my first week, Jo, a 35-year-old mother of two, was admitted with a white cell count of 360, nearly a hundred times normal. She was short of breath and had a headache and blurred vision. I could feel a very large spleen and the veins at the back of her eye were distended and a milky colour. I took her blood for initial diagnostic tests—it was very odd watching it fill the syringe because it was yellowish-white. Blood should never be this colour.

I came to see Jo and her husband. She was in a two-bed bay, but luckily, the other bed was empty. Her husband sat by the bed holding her hand. "As you know, your white cell count is very high. Our initial tests suggest it does look like acute leukaemia," I said.

She didn't flinch: she knew this already and had moved on to thinking about the treatment she would require and what her future held.

I had quite a bit of experience of breaking bad news, but telling somebody they had leukaemia was new to me. "First, we will need to do a bone marrow biopsy to make sure and to confirm the type of leukaemia. It will take a little while to come back, but the consultant should be able to come and talk to you tomorrow morning."

A microscopic examination of her bone marrow aspirate showed she had acute lymphoblastic leukaemia (ALL), a disease mainly occurring in children, with a far more ominous likely outcome in adults. I estimated that a million million $(10^{12})$ cancerous white blood cells filled her blood, occupied her spleen and her bone marrow and that they were doubling in number every few days. Only leukaemia causes the white cell count to be this high.

I was there when my consultant spoke with them. He was youthful but had thinning hair with flecks of grey. He was wearing a tie and a white coat, standard dress for a male doctor in those days. She was by then in a small single room, which contained a standard hospital bed, two vinyl chairs and a sink. He took a seat by her bed and spoke slowly and gently, "Jo, we've looked at your bone marrow aspirate."

"I'm afraid it does show that you have ALL. That's a leukaemia that we can treat, but we are a bit concerned with how high your white cell count is. That makes things harder. There are a lot of abnormal cells to kill. The first thing we need to do is get leukaemia into 'remission', and normally, we do another bone marrow biopsy in four weeks' time to check the response to treatment. Then we can talk about what to do next. We'll start steroids to lower the white count, and then we can commence chemotherapy."

Of course, he emphasised that she was a very young and fit person who should be able to tolerate the treatment well. They had listened carefully and had registered how difficult things were. They were not ready to ask what would happen if remission was not achieved.

Our treatment plan was to selectively kill these abnormal white cells and restore her blood to its normal reddish hue. In 1983, we had far less scientific understanding of this leukaemia and fewer drugs to target the rapidly dividing white cells. We didn't get her into remission: Jo died about five weeks after coming to the hospital. I had a number of sad and intense conversations with this lovely, brave woman and her husband.

Jo was never well enough to go home to spend time with her family although I do have a poignant memory of her five- and eight-year-old children sitting on her hospital bed, one on each side, leaning in towards her. The children were very quiet and almost too well-behaved. When you look after somebody like this, you have to maintain a certain detachment, but the memory of treating her has

15

stayed with me. Jo was the first newly diagnosed leukaemia patient I looked after who died. We did our best, but it was nowhere near good enough.

People with acute leukaemia pose a compelling medical problem. My patients with leukaemia are usually young and previously well but may suddenly have problems that cannot be fixed. Now, using science—the results of clinical trials and meticulous clinical care—we can cure many of these patients, with most returning to a normal life. Communicating effectively with these patients, working with them holistically and keeping them well so that they have a chance of cure: that is my motivation.

Later in my career, I specialised in ALL, researching it for my PhD in Melbourne and my postdoctoral work in London and Philadelphia, eventually becoming an international expert in its treatment, particularly by using bone marrow transplantation. In the 1980s, only about 15–20% of adults with ALL were cured. Over the course of my career, the results have improved so that now nearly 50% of adults with ALL are long-term survivors. As a professor of haematology at Bristol, I have played a part in improving these outcomes. This book tells the stories of some of the remarkable patients I encountered. It also describes some of the experiences and stresses of doctors treating very ill young patients with curable cancer.

## What haematologists do

It's hard to know what the general public thinks of blood specialists. When I am asked what I do, I usually say I am a doctor who does bone marrow transplants and that I look after people with leukaemia. A diagnosis of leukaemia used to be a death sentence, and some may still believe it is, but I think there is awareness that we can now cure many leukaemia patients.

People often comment, "I don't know how you do your job," or ask, "Don't you get depressed? Isn't it very stressful?" Sometimes, it is depressing, but more often, it's rewarding, and it is almost never boring. Few would describe me as an optimist, but when it comes to my work, even I can focus on the positive side of things: the patients we have cured, sometimes overcoming high odds.

Most people know that what haematologists do can be stressful and that sometimes, it is a matter of life and death. As a career, it isn't for everyone. As a professional community, haematologists support each other: we share our successes (there are many), and we console each other about the patients we cannot cure. It is always compelling, and I can honestly say that my colleagues and I are fortunate to have had the privilege of bringing probably hundreds of patients back from the edge of the abyss to live thoroughly productive lives.

To be a good leukaemia doctor, you need to know everything about the disease you are treating: to be totally up-to-date if you are to deliver cutting-edge treatment. You need to keep up with the journals and be quite 'swotty'. For me, this involves reading *Blood, Journal of Clinical Oncology, The New England Journal, The Lancet* and *Bone Marrow Transplantation*. This takes many hours every week. In addition to reading and clinical work, I teach, undertake research and organise transplants and do management, as well as mentoring trainees. Most working days are ten to twelve hours although, with increasing age, I tend to work shorter hours.

Each year, I personally look after about thirty new patients, fewer than most haematology consultants. The complex nature of my patients' problems means that I have very close, intense relationships with them. They are dependent on me, often more than I would like. I make the effort to really get to know my patients because it helps me provide holistic care. As I sometimes say to the junior doctors, I know my patients so well that I may know the name of their cat.

## Go to the cancer centre

After three days of feeling unwell, Dave decided to go to his GP. He was so tired he couldn't walk, and his friends kept telling him he looked pale. His ribs ached, and he had noticed tiny red spots on his shins.

Until the illness started, he was a very fit law student at Bristol University, and he kept telling his girlfriend, "It's just a bad case of man flu. I'll be fine." His girlfriend Becky had Googled his symptoms and was worried. (Google doctor had diagnosed leukaemia—she was scared and didn't tell him this.) "Dave, you've got to go to the doctor."

Because of the pandemic, the general practice was seeing very few patients face-to-face, but the duty nurse, having heard his symptoms, asked him to come to the practice that morning. There were no appointments, but they would fit him in. As soon as he arrived at the surgery, he was sent straight to the GP, who examined him thoroughly; he thought that was a bit unusual. He looked at the spots on Dave's legs and carefully examined his tummy. "I'm not sure what's going on, but we should do a few blood tests. I'll ring you later today when I get the results."

This sounded fine to Dave, and he went home.

Much later, his phone rang.

"Hi Dave, it's Dr Thomas here. The blood tests show a high white cell count and low platelets. You need to go to the oncology centre for some more tests. I think they will keep you in overnight. It's on Horfield Road just next to the Bristol Royal Infirmary."

It was 5:00 pm. He called Becky, who left work and came home to drive him to the hospital. She had pre-packed an overnight bag with toiletries and a change of clothes.

Becky and Dave made their way into central Bristol, squeezing into a narrow space in the car park and shuddering at the sign, which read 'Bristol Haematology and Oncology Centre'. They both knew that oncology meant cancer.

Dave was scared and had not asked the GP any questions; under pressure, he wasn't able to think quickly enough. "Do you think I have cancer?" said Dave.

Becky didn't answer but grabbed his hand, and together they pushed through the revolving doors into the featureless off-white atrium. The person at reception took his name and asked him to take a seat. Becky was holding his brown overnight bag, still in her smart work clothes. Dave was dressed in blue jeans and a black T-shirt (rather restrained for him).

They hadn't been in many hospitals before, so all of this was foreign to them. The entrance was brightly lit, and patients and families waited on uncomfortable chairs beside plastic tables, playing with their phones and drinking tea. There was a simple coffee shop with a limited selection of stodgy British food on shelves (they would later rely on this shop). The lift well lay directly ahead, and (unusually) both lifts were working.

The receptionist came to tell him that he could go up to the ward now. He remembered the instructions: "You'll enter the building on level four; the haematology ward is three floors up, press the button for level seven."

They did just that, got out on the right floor and turned right towards the haematology ward. A smiling nurse spotted them as they were putting hand gel on and introduced herself. "Hi, you must be Dave. We've been expecting you. I'll take you to your room and do some observations. The doctor will be with you in about five minutes."

"Can I come with him?" asked Becky in a soft, lilting voice.

"Of course, you can."

Dave's leukaemia journey had begun.

# Charlie

The day had finally come. Carrie, Charlie's wife, was sitting on his bed in the transplant unit at the oncology centre looking at him, and he knew she was doing this even though his eyes were closed. I entered his room, said hello and told them that we needed to talk.

It was a large transplant patient room with double windows looking out on central Bristol, with room for a hospital bed, a small sofa and an exercise bike in the corner. I pulled a chair up to the bedside and sat down. I was wearing dark trousers and an open-neck plain blue shirt, but I had decided not to wear a plastic gown: it wasn't necessary now.

Earlier that day, a consultant colleague had come to my office and told me that she felt it was unfair to carry on with treatment. "David, I've just seen Charlie. I think we should stop."

I explained to Charlie why I thought we needed to stop active therapy: our efforts had become futile, and his symptoms were such that it was not right to continue with aggressive, life-preserving treatment. He asked how long it would be until he died and then joked to Carrie that she had to promise it wouldn't be any longer than whatever I estimated.

We all laughed. Although I had by this point in my career delivered the 'death talk' hundreds of times, this was the first time I had laughed during it. I then had to ask him a favour. I told him I was writing a book and asked if I could write about him and refer to him by name. I apologised for choosing this time to ask.

Charlie and Carrie said they had no objection, but I wanted to make sure they didn't feel they owed me anything. I noticed that my cheek was wet. I couldn't speak. Crying in front of patients was something I seldom did.

I gave them the options (including continuing treatment for a while, just to see how it felt) and asked whether they wanted people to come and see him before he died or if he needed more time to get his affairs in order. We didn't talk for long; he and Carrie wanted to discuss what they would do. The clinical nurse specialist arrived and stayed with them while they talked. She had been involved from the beginning and was very close to both of them, and they wanted her there as a sounding board.

When I left the room, I felt a sense of relief that at last, we had moved to the final stage of our journey together. He had been so ill on and off for eight years; looking after him had been rewarding but exhausting. Just before I left, he enquired, "Are you alright?" He had seen me cry. Even at the point of dying, he was able to care about how I felt about losing him.

Charlie was in his early thirties and had been battling acute myeloid leukaemia (AML) and the complications of stem cell transplant for about eight years, a quarter of his life. I estimate that for half of that time, he was well, and for about half, he had had significant symptoms that markedly affected his quality of life. He had a good first remission but later relapsed and had a stem cell transplant. That procedure was complicated by a refractory (i.e. unresponsive to treatment) viral infection, but he survived and then eventually relapsed again, about two years later. Unusually, because of the long remissions, we carried out a second transplant, but the time he had after this transplant was a struggle, complicated by graft versus host disease (GVHD),[1] viral infection and liver failure.

It's hard to explain why he was such a special person and why he meant so much to me. Charlie was a tall, very good-looking, blond man, very bright and personable. He was full of life, wanting to live and willing to endure a lot to do so. Even when he was ill, he was able to show he cared about others, including me. (Patients often do ask me how I am, but the focus then shifts back to them. Charlie was different. I was one of the team of people looking after him, but he felt responsible for me.)

His wife, who was totally devoted to him, was a psychiatry registrar; she was always there when it mattered, so warm and lovely to talk to. As a medical colleague, I felt a special duty to protect her and Charlie. Even when Charlie was unwell, he continued to raise money for the oncology centre charity. After the first transplant, when his hair had grown back, he appeared in a promotional video running across the Clifton Suspension Bridge, saying that he was 'running to raise money for Bristol' for the hospital charity and that 'it felt good'. He was smiling as he promoted the charity: it felt so positive.

It took me back to when I first met him and his wife Carrie when he was quite well. He had come to see me about having a bone marrow transplant, including hearing me describe the risks of the procedure. He arrived holding his wife's hand, smiling, but nervous. She was the love of his life.

---

[1] GVHD is an immune disease where white blood cells within the transplanted cells attack parts of the body of the patient (the host), particularly the skin, gut, liver and lungs. GVHD and its treatment can be debilitating.

Charlie lay there, with Carrie leaning over him, holding his hand again, finally at rest. He was a deep, yellow-green colour, and skin was peeling from his scalp like leaves from an autumnal tree. As with many patients who have recently died, he looked somewhat better than he had in the days before: the battle was over. He had taken only two days to die after we moved to palliative treatment.

Nearly all bone marrow transplant patients die in hospital: their care needs are too complex for them to comfortably die at home. I always try to see my patients and their families after the patient has died. It provides finality, on both sides. I often talk to their partner and try to say something useful. We often review the struggle on both sides and how no effort has been spared. It's such an important time.

Most of all, I see my patients after death to remind myself that we need to improve and that we must never be content with the outcomes we achieve and what we do. We must always maintain this attitude; we owe it to our patients and ourselves. I reflected on the things we had done well and less well. Perhaps we had carried on with active life-preserving treatment for a bit too long. I wrote Carrie a short letter about my personal impressions of Charlie. It may have helped a bit.

I thought how much I would miss Charlie: the challenges of looking after him but most of all the pleasure of talking to him. He was such a funny guy. His mother had visited him the day before he died, and instead of saying hello, he told her as she entered the room to fuck off. Not many would joke at this time.

Charlie died on the same date on which his sister had died unexpectedly a few years earlier. Charlie's parents lost both their children before the age of forty, more than anybody should have to bear. Dying on birthdays and death days is common, apparently. Charlie's mother told me this, some years later. I remember my own mother (on her deathbed) saying she did not want to die on her birthday. She died the day before.

In my forty-year career, I have gone to very few of my patients' funerals. I have always felt I needed to maintain a certain distance in order to make good treatment recommendations, including tough decisions at the end of life. At the funeral, three of Charlie's friends told amusing stories about him and his magnetic personal warmth. At university, he was known for looking out for his friends. They also spoke of the change in him when he met Carrie, and of his devotion to her.

I again needed tissues and felt myself well up when I hugged Carrie on the way out of the funeral room. Later, she saw me with a tissue and said, "It was a bit hard not to cry."

Carrie became pregnant about a year later using Charlie's stored sperm and now lives with her little boy, who is the spitting image of Charlie. After many years of living alone, she has found a new partner. I offered to see her after the funeral to answer any remaining questions, but she couldn't bring herself to meet me: seeing my face would have brought back too many difficult memories. I recently emailed her to confirm her consent for me to write about Charlie. She responded, saying that my email made her feel 'quite sad because Charlie didn't want to be remembered for being unwell and having leukaemia'.

Charlie is perhaps the main inspiration for this book. The story of his battle with leukaemia deserves to be told. His ability to confront the harsh and horrible reality of his blood disease, yet retain his humanity, and still live a full life, is something we can all learn from.

# Chapter 1
# Beginnings

I remember my father's death vividly. The six of us were having our usual noisy dinner at the kitchen table. My mother was there, but not eating. The knock at the front door was loud and firm and could not be ignored. My mother looked startled, almost frightened and immediately left to open the door. There was a difficult, deep silence, with us looking at each other. What was happening?

After a while, I went out into the hall. I saw a flash of blue and white, a policeman's harsh uniform leaving, and, for the first time ever, my mother wiping away tears. She came back to the kitchen with her hair tied back severely and asked the oldest four to come into the adjoining study. She said, unceremoniously, "Dad's dead."

My three older siblings, John, Andrew and Jenny, stiffened and then burst into tears.

At the age of eight, I didn't feel anything. "Was he murdered?" I asked.

"No," she said. "He died in a car crash."

We didn't finish our dinner and went to bed early. The following morning, there was a line of bags by the garage door. My mother had spent the night packing up my father's clothes to donate to charity. I don't think she slept that night. The next morning, I remember seeing her in the playroom, talking to my two youngest brothers about the accident.

Unusually, for my non-tactile mother, my brother Bruce, who was four, was sitting on her knee. It all felt so bleak, so hopeless: we knew our lives had changed forever. My mother was left on her own with six children to look after. She never got over my father's death. We would have to be strong.

Both my parents were doctors. I grew up and trained as a doctor in Australia. Three of the six children in my family eventually became doctors, but I was the first. I never really wanted to do anything else, nor would I if I were starting again now. It is the job that best uses my abilities.

It is the most interesting job I could have done, and I believe it has given me the greatest chance of making a difference. As a child, I would see my father come home late at night, tired and unable to spend time with us, but I was not deterred. This is what being a doctor meant in those days although I have tried to be very different with my family. I never really felt I knew him. At times, work had to take precedence and it was an all-consuming passion.

My father and mother both excelled academically (coming first and third in their medical school year, respectively), and my father, a respiratory specialist, was reputedly a 'shit-hot clinician': considered one of the best in Melbourne. So my clearly stated intention to become a doctor at the age of five was taken seriously: nobody ever doubted me because they knew I would work hard to achieve this goal. As a teenager, my academic results were good enough to get into medical school. I did not really need encouragement; I was focused and ambitious. I wanted to be a 'good' doctor, not just 'a' doctor.

My father was forty years old when he died in a car crash. He had driven five hundred miles from Melbourne to a medical conference in Sydney, and on the return journey, his Porsche left the road. He had a colleague with whom he shared the driving; that person was at the wheel when they crashed. Perhaps she was less experienced at driving powerful cars. She survived but was rendered quadriplegic.

His death had profound effects on my siblings and me. At times, the house was a difficult place to live in. My mother looked after us physically but, because of the effects of my father's death on her, wasn't available to us emotionally.

My career goals remained unchanged. In the car were six books that my father had bought in Sydney to give to each of his children. My mother didn't know which book was intended for me but gave me *The Tunnel*, which describes a man escaping from a German POW camp. Inside it, she wrote, "David, Daddy bought this for you in Sydney. Keep it always. Mum."

I still have it. None of my five siblings can even remember receiving a book.

Of my five siblings, my two older brothers, John and Andrew, trained as an engineer and a lawyer, respectively. Both were born prematurely and have impaired hearing. Two younger brothers, Michael and Bruce, trained as doctors. My sole sister, Jenny, is a year older than me and became a social worker. We all got on reasonably well without being very close, and I do remember quite a

24

lot of fights. The family has grown much closer over the years even with me living so far from Australia.

My mum decided to stop working when she started having children. It's worth noting that she had twelve pregnancies to produce six children: there were also six miscarriages. We rarely saw my father. He would leave home early in the morning and return late at night when we were often in bed.

In fact, my main memory of him was seeing him shave in the morning, and sometimes, I remember being spanked by him in the evening when we had been very naughty. Another memory of my father was being taken on long, boring Sunday drives in the country. The six of us would be crammed into a large estate car, with my parents in the front, smoking, usually with the windows closed. It was torture.

We used to regularly stop at the roadside when there was a serious car accident. There seemed to be more car accidents in those days in Australia, and some of them were quite gruesome. I remember more than once that my father certified the deaths of people involved. He considered it his duty to do this, and a doctor's duty took precedence over nearly everything else. Once, my father stopped about fifty metres from two cars that had collided head-on.

He said to my mother as he left to attend the scene, "I might be a little while." It was a typical flat, straight Australian country road. We had been driving for what seemed an eternity; we were bored and wanted to stretch our legs. It was a hot, dry day.

My oldest brother John, who was wearing shorts, started to walk towards the crash. My mother called out, "John, don't go any closer." He returned to the car. We later found out that the driver of one of the cars, who was dead, was trapped behind the steering wheel in full view.

This reminds me of an incident involving my mother, which occurred about six years after my father had died. John, who had recently got his driver's licence, left the house to drive to football training. I remember seeing him leave as he drove down our road to the junction, two hundred metres away. I was back in the house when my mum and I heard an almighty crash. My mum said, "David, come with me."

Worried that John was hurt, we ran towards the crash. I was a fast runner, but my mother found she could barely run because of her heavy smoking. It was a bright sunny day; I arrived there first, out of breath. My brother's car had stopped in the middle of the road, just before the junction. He was not involved in the accident, but he did witness it.

It was a head-on collision, between a car containing two people and a van carrying six young adult passengers, all registered blind. Three people died, and many of the blind passengers were injured. There was glass all over the road. My mum, despite not having practised medicine for years, took part in the initial assessment of the people involved in the accident and gave instructions for people to call ambulances and the police. Medical help arrived in a few minutes, and she comforted the distraught passengers with impaired vision.

John was shocked and returned home, but I stayed to watch. I was about fourteen years old and was not discouraged from doing this; it was a learning experience. I had seen dead people before, and I had seen blood. Many of the passengers had cuts and were bleeding. I watched from the side of the road where I could see the ambulance men carry people away.

It was upsetting, but there was work to be done: people needed to be treated and transferred to the hospital. What I mainly focused on was the systematic way my mother dealt with the situation. I knew I would be able to respond to pressure in a similar methodical calm way. My mum was annoyed that she was unable to run towards the accident and stopped smoking that day, forever.

## Medical school

At Melbourne University, medical school was a six-year course: a relentless grind, with huge amounts of information to assimilate and commonly around thirty lectures per week. It's not possible to enjoy everything you study at medical school. I liked microbiology, pathology and clinical medicine. Most of the rest was necessary but of little interest. These subjects are relevant to being a physician and a haematologist, while much of biochemistry and physiology were not.

Walking out of a cardiovascular physiology lecture, I once commented to a friend that it was the worst lecture I had ever been to, only to find that the lecturer, Prof. Day, was just behind me (he pretended he hadn't heard). In the main, we were well taught, but some of the subjects just weren't interesting. We had to rote learn vast numbers of facts for exams, which we forgot soon after. "Ours is not to reason why …"

More than ten people from my academic private school, Melbourne Grammar, were in my medical school year, and we used to hang out together.

One of my best friends from school, Robert, did not survive past the first year. He didn't want to spend all his time learning boring facts, so he chose to do Latin as an extra subject. There simply wasn't time to do this. He got a first in Latin and failed first-year medicine. He failed so badly that they kicked him out and didn't let him repeat the year.

He then did a science degree and eventually was allowed to return and do a medical degree, about five years later. He just wasn't ready to do a six-year medical degree at the age of eighteen, and with hindsight, he probably should have taken a gap year. The first-year course wasn't intellectually difficult, but we had to spend a lot of time studying. Everybody knew that. When I found out he had failed, I didn't know what to say: I felt a bit embarrassed for him because he shouldn't have failed.

After that, we lost contact. I made some other friends, but I was quite shy and didn't go to many parties. I spent a year living in Ormond and Trinity colleges but didn't really get on with many of the students who went to the pub most nights and only did work before exams. I had lots of other interests, including sport, cinema and travel, but I was serious about my study. For me, medicine was only worth pursuing if I did my absolute best.

The best part of medical school was starting work in the wards as a clinical medical student at the Royal Melbourne Hospital. In those days, one of us was allotted to every patient that was admitted. We were expected to clerk every patient, which meant taking a history, doing a physical examination and getting to know everything about them, including their clinical progress, their social issues and discharge plans. For three years, we were assigned to a 'clinical group' of six students with whom we would spend large amounts of time. My clinical group (Julian, Tom, Peter, Graeme, Sigmar and myself) was intense and competitive.

We would leave the consultants who took us on teaching rounds exhausted by our confidence and desire for knowledge. We would constantly question what we were told, in the spirit of intellectual curiosity. Tom is now a professor of cardiology, leading a major research institute in Melbourne; Julian is a professor and previously chair of surgery at Monash University; and Peter led the Royal Melbourne Hospital intensive care unit for many years before becoming clinical dean. Although it was a very good academic experience, in hindsight, it was a pity to have no women in the group, which would have made our training more balanced and interesting.

About a third of our year group (220 students) were female, and there weren't many all-male groups. I think we approached some women to join the group, but we were probably felt to be a bit nerdy. We talked about medicine most of the time, and our dress sense was probably not all it might have been. We weren't considered a cool group to join.

## Nitya: a patient for all times. Acute lymphoblastic leukaemia: the Empress of all cancers

My paediatric colleagues often refer patients to me who are on the verge of adulthood, usually for allogeneic stem cell transplantation. I love the challenge, but looking after patients in this age group is never easy, partly because paediatric and adult consultants work in quite different ways. Adult haematologists communicate directly with the patient, while paediatricians work both with the child and the parents, who sometimes determine the information that is passed on to the child. We tend to be blunter with young patients than our paediatric colleagues. The transition is not easy for the patient or their families.

I first met Nitya when she was eighteen. It was 2018. She was a tiny Anglo-Indian girl and also an intellectual powerhouse. She and her parents had arrived early for the transplant 'chat', so I called them from the waiting area into the small outpatient room as soon as I arrived. I sat at the desk; behind me was an examination couch with a curtain to provide privacy. They sat on three chairs with her closest to me and her mum beside her.

"Hello, Nitya. It's nice to meet you. How are you feeling?"

'I'm all right' was all she said.

She clearly wasn't. I would need to make an extra effort to connect with her. She wouldn't make eye contact and gave short answers to my questions, often letting her mother answer for her. Occasionally, she looked up and smiled at our clinical nurse specialist Maria, who was perched on the examination couch—the room was crowded.

Nitya's parents were doctors, so I described the transplant in extra detail. To minimise the chance of the leukaemia relapsing, we had to do a transplant where there was a risk of GVHD, the main complication. GVHD could affect most organs in the body and could be life-threatening. Nitya obviously understood this and everything else I said immediately, even though these were new concepts for her. I spoke directly to her, checking she understood.

This direct communication with Nitya was new and different for her parents. Later, her mother spoke with me privately: "I know you have to tell her all about the complications of the transplant, but I don't want her to be too down. I need her to fight."

Both of her parents were NHS consultants from a neighbouring trust. As I said to my colleagues occasionally (in jest), no pressure.

I'll try to describe Nitya. I immediately liked her. Small, very slender, with an instantaneous understanding of everything I said, but prone to episodes of being down, thinking that the gods were against her and turning her head away when given less favourable news. I had to win her confidence slowly. She seemed to prefer female registrars and consultants, and her parents were always there at appointments. I have no idea how they managed, this given their busy schedules. They were nearly perfect parents from a doctor's perspective: helpful, grateful and never interfering. They trusted us.

## Nitya's battle with leukaemia

Nitya was sixteen when she first developed ALL and was managed by a female paediatric colleague with whom she bonded and loved. As is the case for more than 95% of paediatric patients, she was entered into our national paediatric leukaemia clinical trial, went into remission and stayed well for two years. That's when I first met her. Her leukaemia came back two years after diagnosis and remarkably she did her A-levels while having intensive relapse therapy in the hospital. This involved five days of strong intravenous chemotherapy, then low blood counts and a three-week recovery period in hospital.

Again, she went into remission, but there were very small amounts of leukaemia (also called minimal residual disease or MRD) detectable on sensitive molecular testing of her bone marrow. She then received a new antibody treatment called blinatumomab. This made her MRD negative, which augured well for the transplant. If a patient starts the transplant with low levels of leukaemia, the transplant has fewer cancer cells to eliminate and has a higher chance of cure.

Her exams were taken in the hospital school room, in between intravenous infusions and sometimes when she was unwell. She took four subjects and got A*A*A*A. When the nurses told me her results, it made my day and made me realise what a determined young lady she was. The results came out during her inpatient transplant stay. I dropped into her room to congratulate her, but she and

29

her parents were very matter-of-fact about this considerable achievement. I think they had expected these results and preferred to focus on getting through the transplant.

Nitya's transplant was never straightforward. The two things in our favour were that she had achieved a deep remission of her leukaemia and she had a fully matched sibling donor. She dealt with the usual side effects of transplant well but got diarrhoea due to GVHD of the gut, one of the major complications of transplant. This eventually responded to steroids and an immune suppressive drug called ciclosporin, and she was discharged home.

Nitya seemed to be doing well, but I came to work one Monday and was surprised to hear that she had presented to the hospital, with a fever and low blood counts. Tests showed that she had relapsed less than three months after the transplant and had nearly wall-to-wall (100%) leukaemic blasts in her marrow, indicating very active leukaemia.

I was really worried. From the moment she relapsed, I knew she was in trouble. Early relapses after a transplant mean the disease is aggressive and rapidly growing. Until 2018, this would have been incurable: she would have received palliative therapy only and died in a few weeks. However, a new therapy, called CAR T-cells, had become funded in the UK, and my goal was to keep her well enough, so she could receive this therapy. A trial called ELIANA, published in the *New England Journal of Medicine*, of young patients similar to Nitya with ALL, had cured nearly half the patients. Game on.

## The science: How do CAR T-Cells work?

It is important for every cancer patient to understand the technology behind Nitya's therapy (see Appendix 3). Soon, similar therapies will be applied to many common cancers. Chimeric antigen receptor (CAR) T-cells are derived from the same T-cells that mediate the immune anti-leukaemic effect of bone marrow transplants. The patient's T-cells are collected from the blood by a leukapheresis machine and then transported to a special laboratory in New Jersey where they are genetically transformed so that they recognise proteins called antigens on the leukaemic cell surface. In a patient with ALL, when they encounter cells bearing an antigen called CD19, they grow rapidly, increase in number and release chemicals into the blood called cytokines that also kill further leukaemic cells.

These cytokines can have significant, even life-threatening side effects, which may necessitate admission to the intensive care unit. The genetically transformed cells are regarded as a drug; they cost over a quarter of a million pounds for each patient, and as I write only one hundred and fifty British children and young adults have received this funded therapy for ALL. The National CAR-T-Cell Panel, of which I am a member, meets on Zoom every fortnight to discuss each patient and determine suitability. There are strict eligibility criteria, and of course, the patient has to be fit enough to tolerate the procedure. Nitya was one of the first five patients approved by the panel.

My first task was to rapidly wean Nitya off the immune suppressive drug ciclosporin so that we could collect T-cells with normal function, but we also needed to keep her leukaemia under control for two to three months. This was risky because her GVHD could come back as a result of reducing the immune suppression. In adopting this new CAR-T-cell therapy, we were treating patients who in the past would have been considered to be dying, but now we had something to offer them. This was extremely challenging medicine, to say the least.

It was hard to control the leukaemia and keep Nitya well while we waited for the cells to arrive. She had to endure unpleasant symptoms of leukaemia, bone pain and fever; it was not nice to watch her go through this. She needed morphine for the pain but never complained. The two most simple leukaemia therapies (vincristine and steroids) did not work, but I gave her two standard ALL drugs (cyclophosphamide and ara-C), and fortunately, they worked like a charm, achieving a deep remission, good blood counts and much less pain.

Despite her response, her white cell counts fluctuated enormously, and it was a real challenge to leave her with enough T-cells for us to collect and genetically transform. Before successfully harvesting her cells, I had lots of 'what-if' discussions with Nitya and her parents. Her mother, an eternal optimist, kept saying, "Everything will work out."

It was now January 2019. We had to wait over a month for the cells to be genetically transformed and grown in Morris Plains, New Jersey, before they were shipped to a facility in Germany for a quality check. The release of the cells was delayed, and we were worried. Was there a problem? Had they dropped them on the floor? Did they not grow properly? Manufacturing failure happens in about one in ten cases, sometimes because the T-cells were insufficient in number or quality.

In February, we got the all-clear (quality release) late one morning, enabling us to start the gentle 'lymphodepleting' chemotherapy that would allow the cells to 'take' in Nitya. It was very emotional, for the nurses, the patient and her family. We were going into new territory, trying to do the unthinkable. She was the first of about one hundred CAR-T-cell patients we have now treated at our hospital. Everybody closely followed her progress.

Even my non-medical friends asked how she was doing. Simply fantastic! Getting our hospital ready for the first patient to have this cellular therapy had taken hundreds of hours of work from our transplant team, but nobody was counting. The best things in medicine are hard to achieve.

In early February, the cells arrived at the hospital. The bag was labelled with the improbable name Tisagenlecleucel-T and was only about 50 ml in volume. The small bag of cloudy, almost turbid fluid looked as if it couldn't possibly work. But could it?

Her parents looked on, smiling but nervous. The two nurses in the room fussed around, constantly checking her vital signs, almost as if Nitya might explode. The cells slowly dripped through her line into her blood. Imagine that when they entered Nitya's body, they encountered different (leukaemic) cells they didn't like and went on a 'search-and-kill' mission, seeking out all cells bearing the surface antigen CD19, both leukaemic cells and normal ones.

Nitya had some of the usual complications of CAR T-cells, including fevers due to cytokine release syndrome. These problems improved, but we suffered a setback a few weeks later when Nitya developed a most unusual and problematic complication of the cellular therapy: severe liver GVHD, reaching a bilirubin level twelve times normal. Bilirubin is processed by the liver, and the high level indicated that her liver was starting to fail. We were not sure what was happening, but it seemed that the CAR T-cells had eliminated her ALL and then attacked her normal body cells. We did a liver biopsy.

"Nitya, we've got the liver biopsy results back. It does show what we suspected: GVHD of the liver, possibly due to the CAR T-cells. We will have to give you some treatment to suppress these cells. Obviously, if reduce the number of CAR T-cells, we might increase the chance of leukaemia coming back. This is very rare, and I will be consulting with colleagues from around the world."

We had developed a good relationship by now. She looked worried but knew she would get the best treatment.

I sought advice from CAR-T-cell experts in London and Philadelphia, but they had never seen this problem. It's so rare that I and colleagues have written about her case (and those of three other patients) in a scientific paper in the *British Journal of Haematology*. The standard GVHD treatment (including steroids) did not work and had the potential to kill her CAR T-cells, increasing the chance of the leukaemia coming back. The liver tests got so bad that I referred her for a liver transplant.

However, while being evaluated in the liver unit at Kings College Hospital in London, her liver got completely better with a new GVHD drug I had started, called ruxolitinib. It was not funded, so her parents had to pay for it. Her bilirubin went from 250 to 12 (normal is below twenty) over eight weeks. Amazingly, she became so well that seven months after receiving the CAR T-cells, she was able to head off to Freshers' Week at university in September 2019, albeit with a plan to avoid exposure to seasonal viruses. In lectures, she agreed to sit away from the other students and wear a mask, and in her shared student flat, she had to reduce contact with her flatmates, mainly by not using the kitchen at the same time. She never complained about these restrictions.

One of her university supervisors suggested that she deferred her studies, which made her really cross. She told the supervisor, "Why would I want to do that?"

Her leukaemia was in deep remission six months after the CAR-T-cells although she couldn't yet be described as cured. However, she was able to attend university and pursue her dreams. Her parents said they could not thank me enough, but I didn't need to be thanked. Nitya being well was a sufficient reward.

Two years on, I am still actively looking after her, and it hasn't always been easy. Forty-eight hours after arriving at university in London, she developed a fever due to a viral infection and required admission to hospital in London. Her father emailed me in Bristol: "Nitya is in University College Hospital with viral pneumonia."

That increased my heart rate. I thought, *Oh, no. We can't lose her because of a trivial virus.* It was respiratory syncytial virus (RSV), which in normal people causes a cold and a wheezy cough. I called her consultant, a colleague at University College Hospital, who said, "What a lovely young lady. She's not on much oxygen, and I'm sending her home tomorrow. The X-ray definitely shows she had pneumonia." Thank heavens.

After discharge, Nitya and I talked on the phone. I explained again the risks associated with viruses, but she was not deterred: she had faced greater adversity before. She returned to her shared flat and her modified Freshers' Week. "Don't worry, Prof. I'll be very careful not to go near the other students." She was strong enough not to mind doing this or having to explain to other students why this was necessary.

We have followed her leukaemia carefully, with frequent bone marrow tests. On one occasion, about a year after receiving the CAR T-cells, there was evidence of leukaemia being present, which of course I had to make her aware of. This delicate information couldn't be conveyed over the phone, so I asked Nitya and her parents to come to the clinic so we could talk face-to-face.

"Nitya, one of the sensitive tests we did on the bone marrow has suggested there is a very small amount of leukaemia. I'm really not certain if it's real, so let's repeat the test in a month."

She grimaced slightly, closed her eyes and was quiet but didn't burst into tears because she had gone through so many difficult times before. Of course, this made her parents very upset, but the repeat marrows showed remission, so we think this was a false (positive) result.

This new treatment option for patients has revitalised my career. We can now cure previously incurable patients with ALL, and this points to a brighter future of effective immunotherapy for cancer. We can now produce aggressive, genetically transformed T-cells, not the 'lazy' T-cells usually encountered after transplant. It has now been two-and-a-half years since Nitya's CAR-T-cell treatment, and she remains in deep sustained remission. She did very well in her first year at university and was annoyed that it didn't count because of the COVID-19 pandemic.

As she was the first person to receive this therapy in Bristol, she has done lots of TV and radio interviews and is always able to describe her remarkable experiences with an articulate calmness. She managed to live in London in a shared flat and was able to engage in some aspects of university life. Like many students, she has spent a lot of time studying from home, and luckily, she has been vaccinated against COVID although we are unsure if the vaccine will protect her.

For her third year of studying Spanish and Dutch, she is planning to spend six months in both Leiden and Salamanca. This has required quite a bit of planning, but we hope she can do this. We know each other well now. She always smiles when sees me, calls me the more familiar 'Prof' and even finds time to enquire about my health.

# Chapter 2
# Becoming Resilient and
# Learning the Art of Medicine

Looking after leukaemia patients at the highest level requires mental and intellectual toughness, an open mind and an ability to continually learn. Individual patients may be cured, but one should never be content with the overall results: better times lie ahead. The science behind leukaemia and transplant treatment is complex, but so is dealing with the individual needs of the patient in front of you.

My graduation ceremony was at the University of Melbourne on a very hot day in December 1980; we had to wear heavy, dark gowns. There was no air conditioning in the large university hall. My mum sat at the back with the other parents. As I walked on stage to collect my degree, my mother overheard two other mothers saying, "That's David Marks. He did very well—he comes from a big medical family."

The ceremony meant little to me, however: I was focused on starting my career. It had been a long wait.

My first three months as a doctor were in Accident & Emergency (A&E), with my first day spent in the so-called GP section, where I saw about twenty-five patients in a nine-hour shift. Most of the problems were fairly minor and could have been dealt with by the person's actual GP: they didn't require hospital attendance. There were lots of viral respiratory infections and skin rashes. I was told to ask for help if I needed it, but in the main, I was expected to cope. This would never happen now; I would have been closely supervised.

I was confident in my ability to make appropriate decisions, and my memory is that I only asked for help once that first day. I spoke to the admitting officer who told me to bleep the surgical registrar. He was in his eighth year as a doctor and had seen a lot of patients with pain in the abdomen. I was not overawed. "I think he might have appendicitis. Would you mind having a look at him?"

The surgeon spoke briefly to the patient and quickly examined him. "I don't think there's much going on here. Come back if it gets worse or see your GP. Thanks for coming."

The surgical registrar nodded to me as he left. I didn't feel chastened: we were told to get a senior opinion if we were unsure. Appendicitis is commonly diagnosed late, and if it is, patients can get very ill or even die. (Many years later, my own son had appendicitis, which took two weeks and five visits to the hospital to diagnose.) I don't know what the diagnosis was, but the patient did not return to the hospital.

In the 1980s, we were given so much more responsibility than new doctors now. Our first year as a qualified doctor was not preceded by a year of shadowing doctors around the hospital. This was the Australian system, and for me, the lack of a year of shadowing was not a huge problem because my diligent clinical group had already spent long hours in the ward learning how to diagnose and treat patients. The main issue for us as junior doctors was the extraordinarily long hours we worked and the ridiculous rotas of one in three, which represents about ninety-five hours a week. One in three meant working every third night (in addition to the daytime job) and every third weekend.

A weekend on call meant starting at 8:00 am on Friday and finishing at 5:00 pm on Monday, about eighty hours of continuous work. We usually got some sleep in the small hospital on-call rooms, but our nights were never uninterrupted, and we always felt tired. I am not a good sleeper, but paradoxically, this seemed to help me deal with the chronic lack of sleep better than most of my colleagues, who at times found it an exhausting and dehumanising experience.

Despite the long hours and lack of sleep, I loved it. I was doing what I wanted to do and what I was trained to do, and for me, most of it was very doable. The intensity of the work did not come as a surprise to me because my mother and father were doctors. When things were tough, I reminded myself that they had been through exactly the same training. The time I got home was variable, and it was well before the days of mobile phones, so I couldn't warn the people at home how late I would be.

We were meant to finish at 6:00 pm, but it was usually about 8:00 pm before we left. There was supposed to be an afternoon off each week, but that was hardly ever possible. On that day, we were able to leave at about 6:00 pm. The culture was to stay until the job was done: you didn't leave at 5:00 pm and hand over patients.

It was stressful, and of course, I occasionally forgot to do things or made mistakes, but these seldom had significant consequences. For example, once a consultant asked me to check on a patient's liver function tests before going home. Somehow, I forgot and had to come back to the hospital at midnight to look them up (the test results were normal, but it was better to return to the hospital than worry about it all night). I always did my absolute best, so I didn't really worry. I remember constantly writing long lists of things to do and never getting to the bottom of the list.

To me, this exemplifies being a doctor: having lots of 'balls in the air', lots of unresolved problems and many things to remember and prioritise. I unwound by playing football and tennis, watching sports and drinking wine, a long-term pastime. There was little time to socialise, but when there was, it was mainly with other doctors, often just going to get a pizza and a beer. I very seldom stayed out late. Getting enough sleep in those days was an absolute priority.

My general medical rotation was the key job in my internship at the Royal Melbourne Hospital: it was my chance to impress. In my first year, I did A&E, medicine, surgery and infectious diseases at Fairfield Hospital, all three-month stints. The consultants in this general medical firm were two respiratory physicians and a neurologist. The neurologist, John King, admitted three or four new patients a week from his private practice, allegedly to educate the junior doctors.

In fact, it was mainly so that we could do the lumbar punctures they needed as part of their work up and order and chase up the huge number of tests. There were two interns: we shared the workload and covered each other. John King's ward rounds began at 8:00 am sharp, Monday to Friday, every day. He was never late, and we could not be late either. We would present the new patients, talk about and demonstrate the neurological findings and come up with a diagnosis.

These were complicated cases for first-year doctors, so we usually got the neurological signs and diagnoses wrong. Dr King would smile at us, almost in pity, and then demonstrate the salient neurological signs. It was humiliating, but we did learn.

Of the two respiratory consultants, one was Peter Sutherland who took over my father's chest medicine practice when he died. I was quite well-known at the hospital because of my father and was often recognised in the lift by consultants who saw my name badge. I don't think it helped me: I still had to get jobs on merit. Every Thursday, we would have a 'Grand Round' in which we presented the inpatients and discussed one complex patient in detail while everybody ate sandwiches and scones and the ward sister poured tea from a huge teapot. It was very traditional.

All the time we were being judged, and we knew it. Being able to present a complex case succinctly and fluently is a key skill for doctors in training. Researching the diagnosis and the treatment was essential, as they were always testing our knowledge. There were forty interns at Royal Melbourne Hospital (at that time, the best hospital in Melbourne).

Twenty-four got jobs in the second year, but only eight became medical registrars in the third year. It was cut-throat. You had to perform well to survive to year three. You had no choice but to put your career first and not care about the hours you worked. Doctors who didn't get reappointed mainly moved to general practice although some tried other teaching hospitals.

Peter Greenberg was the main consultant on the medical ward where I did my first medical registrar job. He was in his forties, good-looking, with dark, greying hair and a friendly smile. I chose his unit because of his reputation as a rising star. He had specialised as an endocrinologist but was probably the best general medical internist with whom I have worked. However, most of the things I learnt from him were 'soft skills', including how to give patients enough time and the importance of touch.

He would make a point of sitting on a chair by the bed so that he wouldn't be looking 'down' at the patient. Then he would usually take the patient's pulse as a way of physically connecting (although sometimes he found the patient was having an abnormal heart rhythm). I still do this now when I have a serious conversation with a patient.

Greenberg had a habit of being right. He was right so often it was a little bit annoying. On my very first consultant round with him, one of the patients we saw had a known heart murmur and abdominal pain. He diagnosed infective endocarditis (of the mitral valve) and a mycotic aneurysm of a mesenteric artery (infected vegetation broke off from the valve and was carried in the bloodstream to a blood vessel in the abdomen, causing it to weaken). We looked at him in disbelief, but he proved to be quite right.

He was almost always calm. Of course, he couldn't fix everything, but he knew that what he did was the best, most sensible approach and that worrying about things you couldn't fix didn't help. I learnt from that but haven't always managed to be so calm! He trusted his instincts and didn't over-investigate patients, especially when the result of the test wouldn't change things.

At the end of my six months, he called me aside. "David, I just wanted to give you our feedback about your work with us. We were most impressed by the way you managed the patients and how hard you have worked. To put this in context, the last two registrars we've had are the Street brothers, who both topped their year and were outstanding. Your performance is equal to theirs."

This was both encouraging and helpful: I knew exactly where I stood. I give the junior doctors who work with me the same direct feedback.

When I became a professor, I gave an inaugural lecture recounting my career, and I contacted Peter Greenberg for a photo so I could acknowledge him as an inspiring mentor who influenced the way I look after patients. I am still in touch with him. Having retired as a physician, he now works in medical ethics.

## Aisha

Bristol was the first transplant unit in the UK to carry out umbilical cord blood transplants in adults. There are over a million cord units from unrelated donors stored in cord banks around the world. My paediatric colleagues had been doing them for a couple of years; this gave me the confidence to start our own cord blood transplant program.

When a baby is delivered and the cord is clamped before being cut, there is blood in the umbilical cord and the placenta (afterbirth) that is surplus to requirements: this blood can be collected and is a rich source of stem cells that can be used for transplants. I have looked after about seventy cord blood transplant patients, and while the results were excellent, cord transplants are themselves never easy. I have never been worried about being the first to do new things.

Aisha was a doctor in her mid-twenties who had AML. She trained to be a doctor in Cambridge but decided she would pursue a career as a GP near her family. She lived in Bradford, and her parents were born in India. Because of her ethnic background, she had no unrelated donors that we could use as a source of stem cells for a transplant, which was her only hope of a cure. Her leukaemia was in a fragile second remission, and we were in a hurry to find two cord units that were acceptably matched to her. (We use two cord units to achieve a higher cell dose and better outcomes.)

While searching and identifying the cord blood units, she relapsed again; she had to have further leukaemia treatment to achieve a third remission. She is the only AML patient in third remission I have transplanted. These remissions usually last only a few days.

When I first met Aisha, it felt quite intense. She was on her own in the small clinic room. Unusually, she had been referred by a colleague in Leeds because we were the only UK centre doing cord transplants in adults. She was of average height, slight, with dark hair and large brown eyes that fixed on me. "How many of these have you done?" she asked.

I explained that she would be my second adult cord blood transplant patient but that I had helped look after about fifteen children having the same procedure. The principles were the same as any unrelated donor transplant, and other centres overseas were doing these transplants in adults with good results. I am at pains to never conceal information from my patients or 'sugar-coat' the facts. They have the right to be told the truth, but also that way, I gain their trust. I was clear to Aisha that I was on the cord blood transplant 'learning curve', but I was an experienced transplanter, used to looking after very ill patients. She was somewhat reassured but said she had few options.

"I don't have much choice, do I?"

"You don't have to have the transplant, but this is the only way I can think of curing you. I do think it will be tough," I responded. "However, you are a young, previously fit person and should be able to deal with whatever comes your way."

She agreed to go ahead knowing that she probably had a 25% chance of dying of problems related to the transplant.

The cord units matched at only four out of six loci: this was only just good enough to go ahead. We admitted her just before Christmas and gave her pre-transplant chemotherapy and radiotherapy over the holiday period. If we had waited until after Christmas, her leukaemia would have relapsed again. About a week after the transplant, she developed a complication called a cytokine storm with high fevers and had to be transferred to ITU. She then had weeks of fevers, which required steroids, but she got through it.

I was expecting this complication, but its severity surprised me. Later we (using more detailed and sophisticated matching technology) found out that one of the cord units was only a two out of ten match. This was with molecular typing; we wouldn't even think of using this cord unit now.

The severe cytokine storm she had was due to using severely mismatched cord blood units. We were very lucky to get her through this. I remember seeing her every day: her forehead was burning hot, and she sweated freely. Her blood pressure was low, and she needed oxygen and drugs to increase her blood pressure.

After about eight weeks in the hospital, Aisha was well enough to go home. This is a much longer stay than normal, and for most of that time, she was very unwell. Recovery of blood counts is slow in a cord blood patient. She had some GVHD, but it responded to treatment. Before returning to Leeds, to thank me for my care, her mum made me the most delicious lamb biryani, which she brought into the hospital as a leaving present and which I ate with my family later that day.

Her leukaemia has never come back, and she is now more than fifteen years out from the transplant. It is really gratifying that she has been well enough to return to working full-time as a doctor. She lives in Dubai with her husband and is really well, although the total body irradiation has made her infertile. With the aggressiveness of her leukaemia, there's no way we would have had an opportunity to remove and freeze an ovary. That is a sad long-term effect, but it was unavoidable.

I have presented her story at a number of medical meetings, mainly to encourage my colleagues to do cord blood transplants in patients who have no other donors. For these presentations, Aisha allowed me to use a photo of her and her husband walking in the UAE desert, looking well and happy. She is in the foreground in traditional dress, her husband behind her poised attentively, in a sea of white sand and a deep blue sky.

I learnt a lot from looking after Aisha. Looking after medical colleagues requires a different approach. It is hard to look after doctors with serious illnesses, to manage their understandable anxiety waiting for results and give them the right amount of information. Naturally, they are more involved in their treatment than some patients but, in the end, it is best if they trust you.

I always say to my friends with medical problems that they should find the best doctor they can and then trust that person. Sometimes, we continue with treatment for too long, but at other times we need to persist. Aisha reminded me to not give up too easily: many people would have not even attempted to transplant her with those poorly matched cord units.

We are still in touch, and I have recently visited her in the UAE, as a friend. She emails me every year on New Year's Eve. It's so rewarding to save the life of such a lovely young person as Aisha.

## Too late

Jill was a lovely, quiet Physics student at the University of Bristol. She was twenty-three and in the last year of a very productive PhD. She had a long-term boyfriend who lived in Bristol, while she stayed in a regional town because renting a flat there was cheaper. She was well when she went to bed on Friday night, but on Saturday she could barely get out of bed because of overwhelming weakness. She was due to play tennis that day with some friends but rang up to cancel, profusely apologising for the late notice.

Her friends thought nothing of it; they knew it was genuine. Similarly, her boyfriend Tom wasn't too worried when she cancelled their date in Bristol that night. They had planned to go to an Italian restaurant, then for Jill to stay over. He was disappointed and asked if she wanted his company. "No, it's probably a virus; you'll just end up catching it. Best to stay away. I'm going to spend the day in bed."

By Sunday, she was no better, but she also noticed some bruises on her arm and a slight headache. She took some aspirin and it seemed to improve. "Are you any better Jill?" Tom asked on the phone.

"Not really. If it's no better, I'll go to the GP tomorrow."

"Yes, I think you should. This is not like you, but probably the GP won't be able to do much if it's a virus."

She rang the GP surgery first thing on Monday, told them her symptoms and to her surprise got an appointment at 9:30 that morning. "Well, I have to say, you don't look very well, and you do have a few bruises. Your temperature is up a bit, so perhaps it's a virus. We'll do some blood tests and I'll call you later with the results. What's your mobile number? Who lives with you?"

"I live on my own, but I will be at home with my phone."

The blood was taken, picked up and transported by the morning courier to the Haematology Lab at the regional hospital. They did an automated blood count, which showed anaemia and a low platelet count. The laboratory scientist looked at the blood film and thought he could see a blast or two, possibly indicating leukaemia. There was no haematology consultant at the regional hospital that day, so the blood film was urgently transported by taxi to the hospital in Bristol, which took about an hour and a half.

It was looked at by the experienced laboratory haematology registrar, who thought it showed acute promyelocytic leukaemia (APML), a subtype of AML that is considered a medical emergency. The lab registrar called my wife, who was the on-call consultant. She went immediately to the lab, looked at the film and agreed it was probably APML. Jenny rang the GP, asking him to go to Jill's house to tell her that the blood film was worrying and that she should come to Bristol for a bone marrow biopsy and urgent treatment.

We see people with this leukaemia about three to five times a year, and they are at risk of life-threatening bleeding at the point of diagnosis. We have a drug, all trans-retinoic acid (ATRA), which we give to people as soon as they arrive in the ward to prevent them from bleeding. Jenny said to the registrar, "Call to check that we have ATRA in the ward. Do you know the dose?" The registrar nodded. "Give her ATRA as soon as she arrives, and I will come and see her."

Jenny's mobile rang with the GP's number showing. "Have you got hold of her?"

"No, not yet. I'm outside her flat and there's no answer when I knock, and I can hear a phone when I ring. What should I do?"

"Call the police and get them to enter the house: this really is urgent. She might be unable to come to the door." Twenty minutes later the police arrived and, through a crack between curtains, they thought they could see a young woman lying on the floor. They broke through the front door, and she was on the living room floor, dead.

The coroner later found that she had bled into her brain, dying instantly. The GP rang my wife. Both were speechless. They made arrangements to inform the next of kin. Her boyfriend was devastated. Of course, it was not in any way his fault; they made sure he understood this.

Jill had died within six hours of presenting to medical attention. If she had survived long enough to come to Bristol, she would have had an 80% chance of cure and would probably be alive today. There were no obvious medical errors. It was terrible luck that she and her blood film were in the wrong place for a rapid diagnosis. I give an annual lecture about acute leukaemia to Bristol medical students and mention her case as an example of a true haematological medical emergency. When I tell the story, it never fails to make the lecture theatre quiet: the medical students realise that it could have been them.

## Nothing left

I've previously written about life as a junior doctor and the very long hours we had to work. Much of that has changed: ninety-five-hour weeks and being on call every third night are not permitted now. However, don't imagine that life becomes easy when you become a senior consultant. There's more support, and many tasks can be delegated, but it's still hard, and often stressful.

I can't really complain about my transplant clinic being excessively onerous. It's on a Wednesday afternoon, hump day. I usually see ten to fourteen patients, sometimes more when my registrar is away or unable to come to the clinic if the ward is busy. These are complex patients, but I have been doing this for twenty-five years; my non-transplant haematology colleagues see a lot more patients than that, but they are more straightforward. I like this clinic, which includes lots of 'old friends' (people I transplanted a long time ago) and other than being careful and asking the right questions, it's not too taxing. Usually.

The day I am thinking of was different. My clinical nurse specialist (CNS) had to leave early, and I knew I had to see at least two patients with worrying problems. When a patient has a big problem, such as a relapse of leukaemia, after seeing me, the CNS will spend more time with them, dealing with their concerns, explaining things. The CNS came to my office and knocked. "I'm really sorry, David, but I have to leave. My son's got a high temperature, and I have to pick him up from school. My husband's away up north on business."

"Don't worry: I'll cope. We were often in the same position when we had young kids." Actually, I thought, *Oh, no. It's going to be a terrible clinic.*

Clinical nurse specialists play a huge role when we have to break bad news. One patient had relapsed after a transplant for ALL, and I had to talk about subsequent therapy, including CAR T-cells. Of course, this treatment might not work and that would mean they would not survive. The other patient had progressively worsening lung GVHD and was on every therapy available (at least six drugs). If this continued, the patient would eventually die of shortness of breath; a frightening prospect.

The patient's wife wanted to know what would happen when the breathing got very bad. "Can he have a lung transplant?" She had done some research.

45

"Probably not. I did make some enquiries. The lung transplant units don't accept our patients until they are five years out from transplant. That's more than three years away." This wasn't particularly subtle: I was saying that he might not live that long.

Both she and the patient looked dejected. The patient was a plumber who was having more and more trouble doing his job, threatening his family's livelihood. There wasn't enough time to properly discuss this issue, but I said I would email him the contact details of our nurse specialist.

What made the day a lot worse was that I was the attending consultant on the ward and the unit was full of unfixed problems, with the round taking nearly four hours. There was no time for lunch. I had got in early and started the round at 8:15 am, but still had to eat my sandwich while reading the notes of the first patient. My hospital has a small shop on the ground floor with not-very-nice food and long queues, but there was no time to go somewhere better.

The only sandwiches left were Coronation chicken, on tasteless white bread. The problems in the ward meant that my registrar would be an hour late because I had given her mounds of work to do and she 'had' to have lunch (she was pregnant). She called me, saying, "I'm sorry, Prof. I'm going to be at least an hour late."

Again, I said I would cope. "It's fine, but make sure you have some lunch." 'Coping' had become the theme of the day.

I made sure I gave these two complex patients lots of time and muted my phone for short periods to ensure I wasn't interrupted. The patient whose ALL had relapsed had suspected this and was worried about whether the future therapy would work, or indeed if she would get the chance to have curative therapy. I had to rush consultations with the other more straightforward patients: they had about ten minutes each for me to look up their results, write brief notes and examine them, and there was no time for extra questions. I had gone out into the waiting room and said, "I'm sorry: I'm running a bit late and at the moment I am doing the clinic on my own." Some of the patients smiled and understood, while others arranged to extend their parking.

The clinic lasted four hours (better than some), but there were no breaks and not even time for a cup of tea. I apologised to every patient for being late. They didn't complain, knowing how busy I was. One of them said to me, jokingly, "You're always late, Prof. We don't mind."

I think I must have sounded as if I was very stressed: I certainly felt it, with so many problems to deal with at once. The main problem was having to repeatedly answer my mobile, leaving the room to speak in confidence, while also trying to deal with clinic patients. There were further problems in the ward, including a patient who needed to go to the intensive care unit. This took a lot of time and my registrar didn't make it to clinic at all.

After the clinic, I went back to my office to respond to yet more urgent emails and complete some severe adverse event forms for the ALL trial I lead. I went home at about 6:45 pm, with nothing left. The sun was sinking in the sky, but there was good light and only a slight wind. Normally, on such an evening I would go for a bike ride, but I just felt too tired.

I sat down in the kitchen, and my wife, and I looked at each other. I knew not to complain too much about my day and how tired I was; she knew that reminding me of a chore I hadn't done (e.g. emptying the dishwasher) wasn't going to go down well. Equally, talking about a 'fascinating' patient problem wasn't going to be of any interest. I went to the fridge. I opened a bottle of white burgundy and poured us each a generous glass. We talked about that instead.

# Chapter 3
# The Patients Who Taught Me the Most

Managing leukaemia patients, especially with the more complicated therapies, throws up constant surprises. It's seldom easy: the disease, its treatment and the individual personal and social issues of each patient often pose challenges. I am always self-critical in what I do. Sometimes I can see that what I have done is high-quality, but often I can find fault in my management: I feel I could have done better or that I was not quick enough in identifying a problem.

Dealing with patients at a personal level is highly individualised: it can never be perfect. One of the main things is the ability to listen. The patient will often lead you to the diagnosis but more importantly, they tell you what they want.

### 'Please save Jane'

My wife Jenny, who is also a haematology consultant at my hospital, spent a lot of time looking after a most unusual patient called Jane. Jenny used to be one of the attending consultants on the general haematology ward. If a new patient with acute leukaemia was admitted to the ward, Jenny would be her assigned consultant. One such person was Jane. Jane, however, was different. "Mrs Foster, as we discussed yesterday, your daughter Jane does have acute leukaemia, and we are going to try to cure her, but this won't be straightforward."

Sheila, a tall, plainly dressed woman in her sixties, interrupted, "Please do everything you can to save Jane." Jane had quite marked learning difficulties, but no specific neurological diagnosis. She had received some education, but could not read or write. She could say single words but not full sentences, and much of her vocalising consisted of grunts and gesticulations. She was able to communicate her wishes, especially to her mum.

Most importantly, Jane was the centre of her mother's world; she had made lots of sacrifices to look after her. Jane was diagnosed with standard risk ALL and, as we would for anybody else, we entered her onto our national trial UKALL14, our fourteenth national trial of therapy for adults with ALL. (We have recently reported the results of this trial in *Lancet Haematology*; the results are excellent and it is clear that patients benefit from being able to go on this trial.)

As for all young adults, the goal of treatment was a cure, but all treatment recommendations were made to her mother Sheila, with whom she lived. Our direct communication with Jane was limited as she didn't understand what we wanted to do, nor could she consent to procedures or treatment. Jane needed general anaesthetics for every bone marrow biopsy, for line insertions and for four lumbar punctures. Paediatricians treating children with ALL have to do this the whole time, but we don't in adult practice, and our hospital isn't set up for these time-consuming procedures.

Jane was a tall, thin, forty-year-old woman, who initially was quite anxious. We were in a small sterile hospital clinic room with plain furniture. The winter sky outside was cloudy; it was starting to get dark. She was dressed simply in dark brown trousers and a plain T-shirt, with short greying hair. We explained the things we wanted to do simply to her mum, knowing that Jane only partly understood what we were saying.

She was treated with chemotherapy, and four weeks after starting treatment went into remission without major side effects, the usual outcome of a young patient. Jane wouldn't have been able to understand why her hair fell out, why the treatment made her feel sick or why she had diarrhoea. She probably had a 30% chance of cure if we continued with chemotherapy, the standard treatment if you weren't on a trial.

Jenny asked me to see Jane and her mum to discuss whether she should have two-and-a-half years of chemotherapy (with all its logistic problems) or a transplant. At this age, we would normally consider a transplant because chemotherapy is less effective in curing the leukaemia. Jane had a well-matched unrelated donor. She was an only child, so we did not have the option of using a sibling donor. Sheila was a powerful advocate for her child.

"Professor Marks, I want her to have the best treatment, no matter what it is, even if it is hard to deliver." It was very hard to deliver: during her treatment, she probably needed over twenty anaesthetics, some of them taking detailed and time-consuming organisation. The NHS is not always very good at delivering individualised treatment to people with special needs.

"Mrs Foster, I totally agree with you. Our goals should be the same as for anybody else. It's not going to be easy. Much of what we do after transplant relies on patients telling us their symptoms and Jane can't do that."

"I know her really well. I know when she's unwell and when she's not right. I can even tell you about her bowel movements!"

In some of our conversations with Sheila, she was on edge. I think she thought we might alter Jane's treatment because of her learning difficulties. My primary 'contract' was to look after Jane but in this instance, it was nearly as important to look after her caregiver, Sheila.

"Well, in anybody else I think the chance of cure with a transplant is about 50–60%. So in terms of cure, transplant has the best chance but there is also the highest upfront risk. There is a 20% chance of her developing a complication from the transplant that results in her death, and that would most likely occur in the first year."

Sheila looked horrified. You can accept those risks for yourself, but it's harder to do that for somebody else, even if you are their guardian. "It's very important that she takes every drug we prescribe for her. If she doesn't, she could get severe GVHD." I explained that this is an immune complication that can cause inflammation of the skin, the gut, the liver and sometimes the lungs.

"I can assure you that she will take every tablet. I'll make sure she does."

In that respect, Jane was probably more compliant than most patients. The transplant went ahead and was fairly uneventful. Sheila was always in Jane's room and slept there every night for her five-week inpatient stay. She was present for every consultant ward round to answer questions and report problems. For the first two years after the transplant, we did a total of eight bone marrow biopsies and lumbar punctures every three months, all while she was anaesthetised.

Jane was a bit off-colour after these procedures, and we wondered if anaesthetics made her nauseated. We gave her anti-vomiting drugs, but they didn't seem to help. The risk of a single anaesthetic was low, but the risk of thirty anaesthetics is significant. Sheila and Jane had no choice but to accept those increased risks.

Jane is now more than eight years after her transplant and remains in remission, with normal blood counts. We don't need to do any more bone marrow tests, just blood tests which she is used to. She is well and is used to me now. She comes into the consulting room with a smile on her face and laughs when I ask how she feels. Her mum is so pleased that her child has been saved, mainly because of her strong advocacy.

## 'I'm not going to do that'

Roscoe wasn't stupid but some of the things he did were pretty daft. He did warn me from the beginning, the first time I met him and his wife, that he might not do everything I asked. Part of this was wanting to be 'in control' of his treatment. "After all, it's my body, Prof."

'Fair enough', but I wanted to explore this. "At each stage, I will explain the treatment, its goals and the likely side effects. The problem is, that almost everything we do, is necessary and in most cases essential."

He nodded. "Sure, don't get me wrong, I realise you know what you are doing, but for me, it's not just about surviving, it's the quality of my life, and if the treatment is making me feel bad, I might not agree to it." His wife smiled at me: she knew not to contradict him.

"If you let me know about these problems, I might be able to help. At the very least I can explain the reasons for the treatment, or give you medicines to reduce side effects."

"I'll try, but I can't promise."

Ros, as he liked to be called, had ALL, with a high white cell count, and a genetic abnormality that made him harder to cure with chemotherapy. We could get him into remission but probably couldn't keep him there without a transplant.

"Ros, my goal is to cure you. I think we have about a 40% chance, all told. The treatment at times will be tough. I don't really care how we get there, but we must do everything we can to get to where we need to get. One of the main issues is delivering the treatment at full doses, on time."

"Some people are best served by having a transplant. That has some risks but can be very effective. We'll talk about transplant another day because we need to get you into remission first, but we should type you and your siblings now because if they don't match, we will need to look for an unrelated donor and that takes time."

"I only have one brother, and he and I don't get on. We haven't spoken to each other for over ten years. Even if he matched, he wouldn't agree to be my donor."

"The transplant CNS will speak to you about this tomorrow. Very few siblings refuse to donate stem cells. I have seen siblings who hate their brothers donate for them. It's a norm of our society."

Ros didn't let us contact his brother, however. His wife tried to change his mind but couldn't. At this point, I decided not to pursue it.

I'm quite cautious with my patients. Unless we are in a big hurry, I give them time to decide, and I always try to respect their decisions. Ros was different: his non-compliance was quite random and at times he was a pain in the arse. One of the key treatments we use in initial therapy (induction) is corticosteroids (or steroids), which are very important. They made him feel 'hyper' and he had trouble sleeping, so he didn't take them.

I only found this out sometime later—his wife told me as he was too embarrassed to tell me himself. If we had known this, we would have prescribed some sleeping tablets. We also gave him a critical drug called PEG asparaginase, very good at killing leukaemia cells but also with significant side effects. He got some abnormalities on his liver function tests. Ros was a bit of a closet drinker; I was never able to get an accurate alcohol history, but this might have contributed.

The haematology registrar asked me why I didn't confront him about this, and I explained that I didn't want to lose him over this issue. I further explained that, with non-compliant patients, we have to win the war, but not every battle.

Both Roscoe and I were aware of a key moment approaching: when his blood counts recovered, we would assess how much leukaemia he had left. 70% of patients will have cleared all their leukaemia with no minimal residual disease, but those that do not do so have leukaemia that is resistant to chemotherapy and their chance of being cured by standard dose chemotherapy alone is low: they need a different approach. He missed his first appointment for the bone marrow; that was annoying because another patient could have had it. I think he was scared of the outcome. He turned up to the second marrow biopsy appointment, and a week later the molecular test showed low-level leukaemia. I had arranged to meet him and his wife.

"Ros, how are you?"

"I'm OK, Prof. What does the test show?"

"I'm afraid it shows low-level leukaemia, Ros. You have responded, but you are MRD-positive. The best course for us to pursue is a transplant. We will find you a donor."

"I'm not having a transplant so there's no point talking about it."

"I think to make the best decisions for yourself, you need to know about every treatment option."

"Assume I'm not having one. Where do we go from here?"

"Well, there's a new drug called blinatumomab, which has an 80% chance of clearing your marrow and making you MRD negative, but then the best treatment is a transplant because the remission won't be durable."

"Well, what happens if it comes back?"

"It's difficult because the roadmap at that point isn't clear. Standard chemotherapy or inotuzumab and then a transplant because that therapy has no chance of keeping you in remission. We can reserve a transplant for second or third remission, but we might not get remission, and the transplant will be riskier, especially as you won't let me type your brother. The other option is CAR T-cells, but they are not currently available for people of your age. We might be able to get you on a trial."

Ros had listened carefully. "Yeah, I saw a video of your patient who got CAR T-cells."

We gave Ros blinatumomab, five 28-day courses in all. He became MRD negative, which was good, but stopped him from thinking about his disease and confronting reality. He allowed us to look for an unrelated donor, which showed there were no good matches because Ros had a rare tissue type. A year later, his leukaemia returned, with a vengeance. He came to the hospital with a fever, awful bone pain, and a headache.

A bone marrow biopsy showed nearly 100% blasts: there were almost no normal cells. It was frightening to look at. How could we possibly prevail in this situation? We gave him another antibody called inotuzumab, and he went into remission. His cerebrospinal fluid was clear of leukaemia: that was one piece of good news. CAR T-cells were an option but the trial we had open had just closed to recruitment. Again, I arranged to see him and his wife in the clinic.

"Ros, you can do whatever you like. I won't get cross with you, but I will think it's a pity you didn't receive potentially curative treatment. If your brother is matched, I think there's a 40% chance of a cure. If we don't, the leukaemia will come back in the next few months, and this time we won't get you back into remission, and you will die. We will be able to relieve your pain, but it won't be pleasant and it will be too late to change your mind."

His wife finally spoke. "Ros, you can't be like this. Think of the kids. They need to have you around." He looked chastened.

"OK. You can contact my brother, but I am sure he won't agree to be a donor for me."

The CNS contacted his brother, and he did say he would be tested. Predictably, he was a match! He said, "I'll tell you why I don't get on with Ros: he only thinks of himself. But I will donate stem cells. I don't want him to die."

The CNS thanked him. "Ros hasn't decided if he will have a transplant yet, but if he does, we will contact you."

Eventually, Ros decided he would have a transplant. He didn't want to know a lot of detail, but there was no way I was going to transplant him without him understanding the major issues. I was also clear that he would have to come to the clinic and see me every two weeks, and that he had to promise to take the tablets we gave him, particularly the ciclosporin.

"What if I forget to take the ciclosporin?"

"You would be at risk of getting severe GVHD, and that isn't something I would wish on anybody."

I also explained that a little bit of GVHD might be a good thing, as it might stop the leukaemia coming back. Having him in the hospital for the transplant was quite tense: you never knew what would happen next. I felt like I was on a hiding to nothing. If he was cured, well, that was what should have happened. If he suffered a serious complication, that would be my fault, and he would say he shouldn't have had the transplant.

I saw him nearly every day. His wife was there every time I saw him. "Do you know what this is like?" he said, with a croaky voice when he developed mucositis of his mouth and throat.

"Personally, no, but I've seen over a thousand patients with this problem. It looks very uncomfortable, but it is time-limited. Hopefully, it will be the worst thing that happens to you. Let's up the morphine dose: that should work." We discharged him twenty days after the stem cell infusion. Ros was well but had lost some weight. He had diarrhoea during his stay and refused to let us measure or characterise it ('I'm not doing that, no way').

His day 28 marrow showed MRD negativity. I relayed the good news and that we should repeat the test on day 100. I saw him every two weeks in the clinic and things were going well, except that he said he didn't like the ciclosporin. He said it made him feel sick and sometimes he had a headache. We gave him advice about how to deal with the side effects and reinforced the need to take the drug.

About eight weeks after a transplant, he came to the hospital late on a Friday afternoon, after five days of torrential diarrhoea and abdominal pain. I didn't ask why he didn't come to the hospital earlier; it would have achieved nothing. I asked if he had been taking his ciclosporin, to which he said, "Most of it."

Oh, dear! I explained that this sounded like GVHD of the gut and that we would need to do a sigmoidoscopic biopsy (of his colon), but we would start steroids intravenously now. We would also need to measure the volume of his stool (to assess progress) and look for blood and the lining of the gut. He looked resigned to his fate and didn't argue.

His wife said, "This is serious, isn't it?"

I nodded as she fought back tears.

"How long will I be in hospital?" he asked.

"Ros, it's hard to say except to say that the absolute minimum time would be two weeks if you have a brilliant response."

His ciclosporin level was unrecordable: he had been taking very little of it, and what he had taken was not absorbed (we were giving it now intravenously). Again, I didn't confront him with this; we would discuss it later if he got better. Fortunately, he responded, but I knew he would need immune suppressive therapy for months, and for this to succeed, he would have to do 'everything' we asked.

I wasn't certain he was capable of doing so. We tried to think of ways of helping him be compliant. It wasn't going to help giving him a Dosette box for his tablets: when he felt unwell, he didn't take the tablets because he blamed them for how he felt. But this was Ros's nature: he wasn't going to do exactly what anybody said.

In fact, patients not taking the tablets we prescribe is a lot more common than we think, even bone marrow transplant patients. Transplanters do a 'life-saving' transplant and then send the patient home on five to eight drugs, all of which they consider critical. If you prescribe a patient five days of an antibiotic three times a day, most people do not take all fifteen doses on time.

Perhaps unusually, this story has a happy ending. Roscoe's gut GVHD slowly got better; his leukaemia stayed in remission; and he even contacted his brother to thank him for donating stem cells. His brother, who was surprised to be contacted, said, "It's OK. You would have done the same for me."

Ros thought about this, and replied, "Well, yes, I probably would have done, but not really out of the goodness of my heart."

After a year of slowly weaning him off drugs, he was only on prophylactic penicillin, which we give all transplant patients who might have an underactive spleen and are unable to fight certain infections. I saw him in the clinic, and he confessed that he wasn't taking it.

"I'll take the risk, Prof." I looked at his wife, rolled my eyes, grimaced and then smiled.

"OK. I will live with this. I do want you to turn up to the clinic, though." Ros had won the war: he was true to himself and still got cured. Many years later, he is doing well. He comes to the clinic most of the time and sends me Christmas cards with cheeky messages.

Ros is a good cyclist, much better than me; he reminds me of this now and then, and in return, I gently tease him about the cricket. Most of the patients I have cured were just treated properly: they had some luck, and we didn't make any major mistakes. Ros was different: in his case, I do take some of the credit for him doing well. He required enormous patience and a different approach. Getting him through his treatment was far more art than science.

## 'Use the C-word sparingly, if at all'

A long time ago, I used to do allogeneic transplants for patients with myeloma. This was not fashionable then and is right out of fashion now. With all the treatments available for myeloma now, many patients can be kept alive for ten years or more, at very low risk. Myeloma allografts have 20% mortality (or, put another way, in one in five cases you shorten their life).

I saw Anne-Marie with her mum and her sister. She was black, of Anglo-Caribbean origin, with a responsible job. She was in her late twenties, so keeping her alive for ten years with standard therapy didn't seem enough. She wanted a chance of being cured. Cure (the c word) is overused in haematological oncology. For me, it means the disease (leukaemia) goes away, never comes back, and the patient lives long enough to die of something else.

I have seen some patients relapse more than twenty years after their transplant. The transplant was thoroughly worthwhile, but they were not 'cured'. I explained to Anne Marie how the transplant worked (to kill myeloma cells) and how things might come unstuck. With her sister being a matched sibling donor, she had a no more than 20% chance of dying of the transplant; this would be likely due to infection or GVHD, and would probably occur in the first year. If she got past the first year, she would have a good chance of longer-term survival. I don't think I used the word 'cure', as it's not a wise term to use in relation to myeloma, which can come back at any time (although of course at that point all the other myeloma treatments can be used).

Anne-Marie had no partner but listened carefully when I told her that the procedure would very likely make her infertile. "It has a nearly 100% chance of doing this. You might be able to have a child with a surrogate egg, and of course, adoption would be an option."

I saw a tear in her mum's eye, but she said nothing. She wanted Anne-Marie to agree to this procedure and didn't want distractions. GVHD could affect her appearance, and impact her quality of life. Anne-Marie asked some questions but said she wanted to go ahead.

"Anne-Marie, do you have any more questions?"

"Yes, just one: Why am I black?" Extraordinary. I laughed: this joke wouldn't have been to everybody's taste, and some would regard it as offensive. Anne-Marie would remain true to herself.

The years passed. She had minimal GVHD and stayed in remission. Her quality of life was excellent, and she was able to work. She was still single. She lived close to her mum and seemed happy. We monitored her paraprotein every six months, and it was resolutely zero.

Then, about eight years out from the transplant, it suddenly wasn't zero anymore. It was two grams per litre, representing a clear relapse of her myeloma. The result came back about ten days after the clinic appointment; I had to bring her back to another clinic to tell her; this time she came with her mum.

Anne-Marie sat there quietly, looking directly at me.

"Anne-Marie, I'm afraid I have some bad news. As you know, we've been monitoring your paraprotein level since the transplant, and it's always been zero. This last time it was two. I think your myeloma may have come back."

She spoke at last: "Could it be a mistake?"

"It's possible. We'll repeat it, but probably not. There's no sign of the myeloma affecting any of your organs: we have caught it early." I explained that it probably wouldn't need treatment for a while and that all therapies were possible.

"Myeloma treatment has progressed enormously in the last eight years. I'll refer you back to Jenny. She should manage you from here, and I can see you if there are any transplant issues." I would like to have continued to look after her, but now she needed a myeloma expert. I told her I would follow her progress carefully.

She was clearly upset, but she didn't cry. She wasn't going to show any weakness. It was a very sad day. I had seen a number of patients with myeloma relapse more than five years out (five years is normally considered a cure for leukaemia), but this was disappointing. We had prolonged her life, but not gotten rid of the myeloma completely. I have some myeloma patients I transplanted more than fifteen years ago whom I consider 'functional' cures. The myeloma may not come back, and in any case, their lives have been prolonged by so much that the procedure has to be considered a success.

Many years after her relapse, Anne-Marie is well, with controlled myeloma, on oral maintenance chemotherapy. She asks after me ('old Prof Marks'—I will forgive her that). She was not vaccinated against COVID, despite being quite vulnerable. We have spoken to her about this, but she won't change her mind.

Few of her friends are vaccinated; she doesn't trust the people who are recommending vaccination or the people who make them. I have mixed feelings about what we have achieved with Anne-Marie. We have extended her life greatly, but not cured her, and we haven't restored her to a normal life. In my job, you have to accept these sorts of outcomes.

## 'If you supported the Villa, you'd need a drink'

Transplant patients come in all shapes and sizes, and like doctors, they have their foibles. I always take a full social history: I need to know who the patient lives with, whether they have children, what their partner does, and a full alcohol, smoking and drug history. I will see a new patient almost always with their partner, or a member of the family, because that way you get a more complete medical and social history, and often a sense of what is worrying them the most. I normally don't ask which football team they support.

Richard was a good bloke. I couldn't help but like him. He was very respectful and grateful and always shook my hand before and after every consultation. He was thirty-five, tall, with dark brown hair and an athletic physique. His passion was football and being diagnosed with Philadelphia positive ALL wasn't going to get in the way of that.

We got him into remission without undue trouble; he then had a transplant and that went well too. After all, he was in his mid-thirties and pretty fit from playing five-a-side football in a local competition. However, he got liver GVHD and needed a liver biopsy to confirm the diagnosis, followed by many months of immunosuppressive drugs. I was seeing him frequently, checking the liver function tests and gradually reducing his steroid dose. Then, without warning, he disappeared and was completely uncontactable. Our CNS emailed him and phoned him repeatedly.

His absence was during the (football) World Cup: Dick had gone to London with his mates to watch football in the pub, nearly every game of the World Cup. In the middle of the tournament, he travelled to Russia to watch some games involving England, taking his drugs but also drinking plenty of beer, interspersed with shots of vodka (not a good thing to do when you have proven liver damage). He was absent for nearly seven weeks.

When he returned from the World Cup, his liver improved, so I was able to wean Richard off steroids. Unfortunately, he then again developed abnormal liver function tests, the cause of which was not clear. My registrar organised an ultrasound, for which he didn't turn up (this wasn't his fault; they didn't send him the appointment in time, although he did get a nasty text telling him how much money he had wasted by failing to attend the ultrasound). At the next appointment, I took a proper alcohol history. He had previously said he drank two pints of beer twice a week; by the time I had asked the right questions, it was two nights of drinking five pints, with two double whiskies. He then admitted it depended on whether football was on the TV and how Villa was doing.

"Prof, most nights I spend at home with the missus, and I don't touch a drop. When my team are playing, I watch it with a mate at his house, and we'll always have a drink."

"Richard, it's fine. I just need to know how much you drink, so I can give you the right advice. Just for the record, I like football too and I'm not a teetotaller. I'm not going to advise you to totally abstain."

I asked him to drink minimal alcohol for one month and then we would measure his liver function tests and see if we needed to re-biopsy him. That night, Villa lost 1–0. I'm not sure that his abstinence would have commenced that night. Villa was promoted that year but is now in the Premier League, so there will be nerve-racking times ahead for Richard and his liver. He misses most of his clinic appointments, but he is alive and well, so that is good enough for me.

## 'No treatment, thanks'

Kate was 65. She had a husband, with whom she had made a conscious decision to not have children, preferring to pursue their careers. Before coming to our cancer centre, she was well, hardly ever going to the doctor. For three weeks, she had been tired, almost unable to do her morning bike rides. Something was wrong. She had lost some weight without trying.

At first, she enjoyed the weight loss; then it worried her. In the morning, there was a slight dampness to the sheets, and she felt a bit achy. Her self-diagnosis was hypochondriasis; a big case was coming to court, and she was the one calling the shots. She was wrong: she had a serious illness.

Kate called the GP about her symptoms and was surprised to receive a call offering a face-to-face appointment one hour later. "Kate Smith, please go to room five." She got up from her plastic chair in the spartan, functional waiting room, and walked up the stairs to the room with a five on the door. Even going up the two flights of stairs to the consultation room made her feel short of breath.

"How long have you been unwell?" asked the GP, noting her pale colour.

"About three weeks," she replied, thinking that she hadn't been in tip-top shape for a while. Her Strava times on the bike had been terrible, with very few PRs.

"Anything else?" said the young, smartly dressed GP.

"I suppose I had better have a look at you. Pop on the examination couch. Leave your shoes on." There was nothing to find, but her spleen was enlarged, and she was definitely pale. "I don't know what this is. It could be a virus. We need to do some blood tests, and I will look for glandular fever. Your spleen is a bit big, but that could be due to lots of things. I'll call you later today with the initial results. If I were you, I would have the day off work."

That last comment was what really worried Kate. The GP watched her grimace and regretted asking her to have the day off—it only caused anxiety. What harm would working do? The GP had seen three patients with 'colds' and was thoroughly bored. This was the opposite of boring: she was worried.

The urgent bloods came through at 3:00 pm, and she called Kate. "All your blood counts are a bit low. Your marrow isn't working properly, and they want to see you in the haematology unit." She didn't mention that there were a few suspicious cells on the blood film that could be 'blasts'. She didn't think that was her job; that was for haematologists.

"Hi Kate, I'm Dr Farr-Jones, the haematology registrar. All your blood counts are low, and we need to do a bone marrow biopsy."

"Is it something serious?" asked Kate.

"It could be. We should have a result by mid-morning tomorrow. Perhaps ask your husband to come in?"

Her husband arrived at 9:00 am, and they waited together for the consultant to arrive. He was older-looking, with short hair, an open-necked shirt and creased trousers. He grabbed a seat and pulled it to the bedside. Kate was a well-presented lawyer, thin, simply dressed with short blond hair. Her husband wrote everything down.

"Hi Kate, I am Professor Marks, one of the haematology consultants. I have some news. I'm afraid your bone marrow test shows that you have acute myeloid leukaemia." The rest was a bit of a blur. She remembered afterwards that I had said there was probably a previous marrow condition called myelodysplasia, and that we would know more in few days when we got the genetic tests back.

Kate spoke first. "I'm kind of gathering that this type of leukaemia has a low chance of cure."

"The full genetic markers won't be back for a week. We'll know more then."

"Do I need to make a decision about treatment now?"

"No, we could send you home and see you in the clinic when we have the results. Just as a precaution we should take some blood and start to look for a donor for you, as it's likely you will need a transplant."

She said she would try to keep an open mind, but her current thinking was that she would not want a transplant. I didn't ask why because it was frankly too early to have a definitive chat. Her husband got it (he had a serious look on his face) but was strangely quiet. I got the impression that they would talk about it at home, but his wife would make the decision, and he would have to live with it.

"I will see you in my transplant clinic in seven days. Your counts are OK, but let us know if things change."

"Can I have a glass of wine?"

"Sure, just one or two."

I was running late when they returned; they were already seated in the clinic room with the clinical nurse specialist Maria. She passed the time by talking about what Kate and her husband had done in the last week. The answer was not much: they were too worried about what the future held and the impending decision.

"Kate, how are you feeling?" I asked.

"I'm ok, no real change. Not sleeping great. I'm tired, but it's hard to say what that's due to. I have done quite a bit of reading, and I have spoken to my GP about what I should do."

"So, the news is not good. You did tell me not to sugarcoat things. You have complex cytogenetics (that's more than five chromosomal changes) and what we call a monosomal karyotype." Kate had read about this and said so. "Added to that we would need to do a transplant using a cord blood donor or a haploidentical donor because you have a rare tissue type. Our unit routinely performs these transplants, but there is a higher risk of dying compared to using a sibling or unrelated donor."

Kate had a lawyer's mind and wanted to cut to the chase. "From this point, what do you think my chance of cure is?"

I was prepared for this question. "5–10%. We have a 50% chance of getting you into remission. That will take four to five weeks before we know, and you are likely to spend most of that time in hospital, and for some of that time, you are likely to be unwell. There is a 5–10% chance of dying during that first month. If we get remission, you will feel well."

"If I get a remission, how long will it last?"

"Six to nine months on average. You would need one or two more courses of chemotherapy, and some of that treatment would be in the hospital."

"What's the chance of not getting through the transplant?"

"About 25–30%." She grimaced; she didn't like the sound of that. She looked across at her husband, who was wiping a tear away. He knew what was coming.

"I have thought about this carefully, and I have decided that I'm not going to have any chemotherapy. I'll have transfusions while I am well, but when I become unwell, I will stop all treatment. Can I please see somebody in palliative care?" I spoke with them, trying to make them understand the impact of this decision.

Very few people decline all treatment: most want their life extended, or at least to give things a try. However, Kate's reasons were sound. She had very little chance of cure and treatment would not give her much good quality time out of hospital. She was reasonably well now and could be at home with her husband.

She wanted some time to talk to her law firm and hand over some cases. I had nothing but respect for her and certainly didn't try to twist her arm. I felt sad about her decision and powerless to do something useful to help her. She deserved to live into her old age, but that wasn't going to happen.

Kate died about seven weeks later. She only needed blood transfusions for the last three weeks, which required twice-weekly visits. Her bone pain was relieved by morphine. I saw her now and then in the day unit, checking that she was OK. Her husband was with her, often holding her hand when I visited.

She would smile when she saw me, constantly thanking me for her care. To my mind, I had done very little. She died in her sleep, with her husband beside her. He emailed me to tell me she had died. I wrote to him to tell him how brave she was, how much I liked and respected her and the decision she had made.


## 'Don't give up on me'

Sally's leukaemia kept coming back. She was diagnosed with ALL when she was twenty. At that time, she was a medical student at Cambridge University, but her family lived in the country outside Bristol. I and my colleague both looked after her. She was a tall, striking blonde woman.

She had to defer her studies for a year but to her credit was able to resume them while she received two years of low-intensity, maintenance chemotherapy. This was not easy because once a month she felt quite unwell for three or four days and there were lots of hospital visits and blood tests.

She had a serious boyfriend who went to the same college; he was studying law. She missed him terribly when she was in Bristol, and he was in Cambridge. In spite of the five-hour journey, he visited her frequently, and they stayed together. He then moved to London to finish his legal qualifications before accepting a training contract at a Magic Circle law firm.

She completed her studies—this coincided with finishing her leukaemia treatment—and got a job as a junior doctor rotating through the best London hospitals. She lived with her boyfriend but because they had such busy jobs, they didn't see each other much. I asked a colleague in London to keep an eye on her, but she preferred the continuity of seeing us for regular follow-up visits.

She relapsed four years after diagnosis. Transplant offered her a good chance of cure, maybe 50%. We got her back into a deep remission and when she was admitted for a transplant, she looked really well. She got the usual symptoms that total body irradiation causes such as bad oral mucositis requiring opiates, but basically sailed through the transplant and was home in record time. It's different looking after doctors, but she remembered the transplant as 'not too bad' and commented, "I was much more ill at times after chemo." This positive memory of the transplant turned out to be important.

Everything went well: she had no GVHD and went back to being a junior doctor, a remarkable outcome. I saw her infrequently because she was so well. Two years after the transplant, on a routine blood test in the clinic, she had low blood counts and leukaemic blasts in her peripheral blood. Her second relapse. Nowadays she would have had CAR T-cells, but they were an unproven therapy at the time and unavailable in the UK.

I explained what a difficult position she was in. She had done her research, and said, "Prof Marks, I'm really well, and I don't want to give up. Why don't we do a second transplant with a different donor? I tolerated the first transplant well and didn't get GVHD, maybe I will with a different donor."

I had done very few second transplants for ALL patients because there was little evidence they worked. But in a way she had a point: she was well, it was a late relapse and as she said, there were ways of doing the transplant differently to try to achieve a better outcome.

"Sally, let's explore this. You do have lots of potential donors. If you remain well and get a deep remission, it's something we can do but the chance of success is low, and we have a one-third chance of shortening your life. Second transplants are very toxic; there is a high mortality."

I was surprised by the bluntness of her response: "Prof, you're a long time dead."

This was her only chance of survival, and she was not ready to die. Her partner, now her husband, winced, then reached for the box of tissues. The conditions for proceeding to transplant were met: we did the second transplant, with less intense chemotherapy. Again, she got through it well and was in remission six months later, asking if she could return to work.

I said, "Sure, if that's what you want to do, but don't be too hard on yourself. Take time to recover and avoid patients with viruses." For the first time, she looked like a transplant patient: thin, with incomplete hair regrowth this time, with a tinge of premature greyness.

A few months later, she called me from London. "Prof, I think I've relapsed. I'm really tired, and I feel a bit achy. I want to come and see you; you know what I'll be asking."

"Sally, come to the day unit tomorrow morning. We'll do a blood film right away then I'll see you. Can you bring your husband and your parents?"

I don't like keeping people waiting with the sword of Damocles hanging over them: Sally wouldn't have slept much that night. Her blood counts were low, and the blood film had lots of leukaemic blasts. This was her third relapse. We booked a big clinic room because I was accompanied by our leukaemia CNS, and Sally came with her husband and both parents as requested. I explained that the leukaemia had come back and that another remission was unlikely, but even if we got one, there was no therapy to give her that would keep her in remission. She wasn't eligible for trials of two new targeted drugs, and the CAR-T-cell trials being run in America were not accepting non-US patients.

"You won't do another transplant?" I shook my head.

"It wouldn't work, and it would reduce the quality of the time you have left. I'm really sorry." Her husband and parents were quiet: they had expected this. "Our palliative care nurse will come and see you. Are you going to stay in Bristol?"

She nodded. Previously, she had said she didn't want to be seen by palliative care: for her, it was giving up. I learnt a lot from Sally and her indomitable spirit. It taught me to not give up too easily but also that there does come a point where stopping active therapy is the right thing to do. I was sad when Sally died, but knew that we had done our absolute best.

# Chapter 4
# People in Medicine

You meet a lot of different people in a forty-two-year medical career. I worked for ten years in Australia, three in Philadelphia and the rest in the NHS, interacting with doctors, senior nurses, students and managers. Working in the NHS can change you: facing intolerable pressures day in, day out is hard and can blunt one's humanity.

We all have to behave a bit differently at work compared to home: we have to be 'professional'. We often can't say what we think, and we can't just give up either. Clinical patient-facing doctors are a self-selected group and are not the average person you meet outside medicine, whereas senior managers are harder to characterise as they vary enormously. I have some tales to tell.

## The medical student

It was September 1983, time for the final year medical exams, and as a second-year doctor at the Royal Melbourne Hospital, I was asked to help with the clinical exam. The major component was spending an hour with a complex patient with multiple medical problems, then presenting the history and physical findings to two examiners, with an ordered problem list and a treatment plan. My job was to look after the patients that day and to check and document the physical examination findings that the students had to uncover in order to pass.

Two senior consultants sat at a table in the ward 'clinical room' with the candidate in front of them and me off to the side as an observer. I had done the final clinical exam myself only two-and-a-half years earlier. The room was white-walled and sterile: there was a blackboard and a small window, but no decorations or furnishings to make it comfortable or welcoming. The chairs were made of plastic, hard and uncomfortable.

About midway through the seven-hour session, a young man called Tom entered the room to present his 'long case'. He was tall and very thin, with untidy hair. He was visibly nervous, but that wasn't unusual. He did not quite connect with us; there was no eye contact, and he did not respond to us wishing him 'good morning'. He presented the history of the patient he was assigned but didn't mention any of the main problems the patient had. We were worried. Almost nobody in their sixth and final year failed their exams.

The examiners gave him some prompts, but he didn't take them and seemed to answer different questions to the ones posed, or barely answered at all. The examiners looked at each other and appeared to be asking, "How can we turn this around?" They wanted him to pass.

Eventually, one said, "Tom, what were the main problems for this patient? What did you think about his cardiac issues?"

He didn't respond.

Then I noticed his tie. In those days, male medical students wore trousers, a plain shirt and a tie, and a short white coat, much shorter than the long coat qualified doctors wore. Nothing too bright, or anything that would make you stand out. Tom's tie was a sea of purple and green and had black animals and demonic figures on it. Heaven knows where he got it from: it seemed to be a pictorial representation of the contents of his mind. Further gentle questioning made it clear that he was probably psychotic; there was a pane of glass between us. The room became quiet and there was a palpable sadness as he left the room.

Tom failed; in fact, he barely scored at all for that long case. Immediately afterwards, he was referred to a psychiatrist who diagnosed schizophrenia, and he never became a doctor. His friends and his clinical group were questioned, and they said he had been like this for some time. (Clinical groups are together for three years.) They had helped him with exams, and somehow, he scraped through.

He was quiet on ward rounds, but nobody made much of it. Poor fellow, having his fragility so cruelly exposed by the stresses of the final exam must have been tough, but it could have been worse. Imagine if he had got through the exam. Just think how much trouble he could have caused as a junior doctor!

Of course, this should have been noticed long before the final clinical exam. It did not reflect well on our supervision or the pastoral care of medical students in the late 'seventies. Nowadays, Tom would have had a mentor or a personal tutor, to whom he would report regularly. In those days, there was minimal individual supervision. In this unforgiving environment where only the fittest survived, if you had a personal problem, you just had to get on with it. Six years of enduring the rigours of being a medical student was regarded as good preparation for what was to come.

## A tale of two managers

The big, lumbering orthopaedic surgeon had somehow become the boss; it was 'his turn' although he had long fancied himself as a senior manager. The most senior clinical managers at the hospital were seldom outstanding clinicians: they wanted to spend their time doing other things, or they were burnt out. The trust preferred obedient, not-very-bright people to be managers, who would act in a corporate way and not question too many decisions.

George was a surprising person to deal with, completely uncompromising and determined that his little corner of the NHS would be totally unenjoyable to work in. Nobody would get what they wanted to do their job better, and everybody's word or opinion would be doubted. His default position was that everybody was trying to swindle the NHS and waste money.

He had a strangely camp voice, taking too long to say things and constantly using flowery language. He was full of what I call 'NHS speak': 'cost savings', 'disappointed' and all the other clichés, including my pet hate 'we are facing a big challenge'. When resources are clearly inadequate—when you know you can't do something properly or safely, and there's no sign of extra resources being allocated—this isn't a problem, but a 'challenge'. That's just fucking stupid. Why not call a spade a spade? Just carrying on (when we can't succeed) is what we always do, and it doesn't work.

NHS managers should stop using this ridiculous word. On many occasions, he was just plain obstructive. One weekend on call (looking after thirty-five very ill haematology and transplant patients), I was rostered on with three junior doctors, all of whom called in ill. We could only get one locum doctor to cover, who did not know the patients and had minimal experience in haematology. This—looking after vast numbers of patients with no help—was a 'challenge', according to George.

I asked for another doctor and my request was escalated up to George, who said that the hospital was limiting the number of locums they could pay for, and he wasn't going to approve the expenditure. It made me feel like screaming. Instead, I went to my office to vent, wondering what on earth I could do to make the weekend safe. We got through it, just, but only because I worked sixteen-hour days and did the junior doctors' duties as well as my own. I was called constantly through both nights. I had almost no sleep and then had to front up on Monday.

I recall another encounter with George, while I was Director of the BMT unit. The unit was expanding, undertaking more transplants and offering more people curative treatment. We would soon be doing CAR-T-cell therapy, which would require more resources. Our transplant results were excellent and our unit made a huge income.

We needed more beds so we could admit all our patients to the transplant ward, but with the current provision there were delays to treatment and our patients were being housed in wards with staff that did not have the training or experience to look after them. This caused untold distress to our patients, and we were running around all over the place, trying to look after patients in wards where the staff didn't understand specialist transplant problems. The treatment delays mattered: some patients relapsed and could no longer be cured.

I had made an appointment to see George and knocked on his door right on time. He was sitting behind his desk, wearing a dark grey suit, a blue shirt and a red tie. His hair had comb marks and a very straight parting. Very few doctors dressed like this anymore. He knew from my email requesting the meeting he would be challenged, but he was not going to concede anything.

He didn't invite me to sit down, but I found a chair anyway. He looked up at me with a bored expression, indicating that whatever I said, it wouldn't change anything. I had come prepared and the day before had sent him a detailed email about the issues, giving reasons for the proposed changes, and financial justification.

"Good morning," I said.

He only grunted in response. It was morning; he couldn't deny that, but it certainly wasn't good.

"Hopefully you've had time to read my email."

He nodded.

"I'd like to explore increasing our bed provision."

"Why do you think your unit is more important than any other part of our division?" Full-scale attack. Not passive-aggressive: just aggressive.

"I don't. But this does need to be addressed. This problem won't go away. The delays our patients are experiencing may be affecting their outcomes.

Because of the bed shortage, we're constantly having to rearrange transplants, including stem cell donations from international donors."

There was no point arguing with him: he would prevail. I felt very angry, but I couldn't show those feelings and give him the upper hand. I left, saying that I would be revisiting this issue; that it was about patient care; and that I couldn't let it go.

The response of this manager to every request was 'no' or 'I'll think about it', which meant 'I'll come back to you in a while to say no'. His dominion also included the oncology ward, which was one of the worst wards I have ever experienced: a throwback to the sixties of antiquated, four-bedded bays, shared toilets with no privacy. These were dank, crowded conditions that somehow made having cancer even worse.

Nothing was done about it until the charitable body of the hospital could stand it no more and raised the money. They then 'had' to plan an update of the ward, although it still hasn't happened because of COVID. This was enforced change that should have taken place decades ago. In the meantime, the managers took credit for the ward update they had almost nothing to do with and had obstructed for years.

I remember a final encounter that typifies George. We were discussing some necessary changes to the BMT unit to make our outcomes 'world class'. He politely listened, occasionally nodding: he seemed to be on board. Then he interrupted to say, "OK, David, thanks for telling me about these plans. What would you say if I told you that we can't afford for you to be world-class? That we should aspire to something less?"

I looked at him, I couldn't tell if he was joking or just being annoying. What was proposed was not expensive: it would pay for itself because it would improve efficiency and bring in more income. I was really cross, but initially said nothing, remembering my mother's maxim that 'if you have nothing nice to say, say nothing at all'.

Eventually, before leaving I said, "I don't have any interest in being second-best. Our patients deserve better than that."

He had won, as he always did. We could try to develop the unit, but it had to be in ways that did not involve this manager. George wasn't the worst manager I have come across and, in many ways, he was typical: someone who 'enjoyed' being mean with resources and thought that this meant he was doing a good job. It didn't. Doing a good job in the NHS means changing things and improving things. Why can't we get rid of these people? Because they are part of the culture of the NHS.

The second manager who springs to mind, Peter, was a senior person from finance with whom I had dealings over a period of about twenty years. I had to do battle with him every time I needed a new colleague. Every time, we would write a detailed business case, showing that transplant numbers had increased (bringing in more money) and that the existing workforce couldn't cope.

We benchmarked against other large units and showed we had fewer transplant consultants per patient transplanted. He would meet us (I give him credit for that) and agree that we needed an extra person, but then stall by asking for additional information. At one point, I was the only transplant consultant in the UK looking after thirty new transplant patients a year. I was run ragged, but he wouldn't accept it.

I recall a meeting that included our BMT unit manager, who supported the business case. Peter was different to other financial managers. He entered the room breathing heavily, shirt hanging out, exposing his hairy midriff, his tie to one side and probably with food stains on his shirt. He had a scruffy beard and usually smelt of daylong sweat.

"Hi, Peter, I hope you have had time to read the business case?" This had taken hours to write, all after hours, often about twenty pages.

"I've read it, and I agree you are doing more transplants, but you haven't shown me that you need an extra consultant."

"We've benchmarked against four other units. We have by far the lowest consultant to patient ratio. It's not safe." (When you raised the issue of safety, they had to listen.)

He wouldn't say 'no', but I am not sure I ever heard him say 'yes'. Apparently, he used to say 'I never say no to a good idea' to his colleagues in trust headquarters, which must mean that I never had a good idea. Over my career, I managed to persuade the hospital to appoint three new consultants, but every time it took more than two years of arguing. Many people gave in, but I don't do so easily. However, every time it made me extremely angry, mainly because I had to be civil to him in the meantime.

I never accepted this style of management: not good enough is never good enough. My patients come to me for the best, absolutely world-class treatment. Why should they settle for less? I constantly asked for resources, more nurses and doctors, better drugs (including some that were not yet approved), a better place to work and a better environment for the patients.

## Rachel

I first met this short, blonde, Welsh doctor about twenty years ago. I was giving a talk in London about haploidentical transplants, as our unit had just done the first adult 'haplo' transplant in the UK. I didn't notice the intense junior doctor in the audience, taking notes, but she remembered me. She and her partner wanted to move from London, to be closer to their families in Swansea. She wanted to specialise in bone marrow transplantation. Bristol was the perfect place: the perfect distance from both sets of parents, close enough to deal with problems, but not so close that they could just drop in.

One day I took a phone call from my friend Jamie, a consultant at Bart's. He began with a hard sell. "David, I have a haematology registrar we have just appointed who wants to move to the South-West Deanery. She was by far the best haematology SHO [senior house officer] we have ever had, and she wants to be a transplanter. We are very sad she will be leaving us." I had little influence but said I would do my best to facilitate her transfer.

Rachel interviewed very well and secured a training place in Bristol; she always prepared really thoroughly for interviews, leaving nothing to chance. I met her for the second time on a weekend on call. She liked looking after ill patients: nothing worried her. She was interested in every detail and stayed around until the job was done, rather than downing tools at 5:00 pm. She was a little old-fashioned in her approach to medicine but in a good way.

However, it was when she started in the transplant unit that she really captured our attention. Like many doctors, she had some mild eccentricities. Perhaps the most distinctive thing about Rachel was her gait: you could always hear her coming. She wore heels and was always in a hurry. It was a distinctive, rushed clatter on the floor—you always knew when she had arrived.

Her mild Welsh accent became more heavily Welsh when she got excited or more demonstrative. I have informally advised or mentored her for a long time, talking her through some difficult situations with patients. When one of her patients is dying, she is affected by this but also tough enough to get through it. Rachel was keen to learn and had a strong work ethic. She listened and was respectful.

From the very beginning, she positioned herself to be able to be appointed as a transplant consultant. She knew she needed to do a relevant research degree, and found an immunologist to take her on. She did a good PhD and became respected as a junior scientist when presenting her research at European meetings.

Rachel came back to clinical work and soon after became pregnant. This wasn't good timing because the consultant interview was coming up. She did the interview less than two months after having the baby. She was tired and her brain wasn't in the right space, but as usual, she prepared well. A consultancy interview follows a set format: 'management' questions come from two of the panel, usually at the end of the interview.

She did the Hammersmith Hospital consultant interview course and answered the management questions better than anybody could remember any candidate ever doing. The trust representatives on the interview panel couldn't stop smiling; they absolutely loved her. As I write, she has, unsurprisingly, just become a senior clinician manager in the trust. Before I retired the tables had turned: she was now my boss.

## Dr Jekyll or Mrs Hyde?

We all adopt different personae at various points in our lives. The professional relationships we have with colleagues are distinct from those we have with our families. At work, we have to be fair, objective and sometimes quite detached. We can rarely be emotional, or if we are, we reserve it for certain situations.

I work with a palliative care consultant. We have a good working relationship, with lots of mutual respect and similar views about end-of-life care. (Cancer doctors are sometimes slow to move to palliation.) When we see each other, we say hello, smile and chat, often about non-medical matters. She is an excellent colleague who improves my working life.

Her husband is a radiologist at a different hospital, with whom I had worked as a junior doctor about twenty years ago, and he had agreed to review an X-ray for me. I mentioned in an email that I hadn't seen him for some time but that I saw his wife regularly, and how nice she was to work with. He replied saying that he would pass on the compliment, commenting in passing, "I guess she reserves her angst for home." Although there was levity in his response, it also spoke the truth. Which is the real person?

Both, I would say, but perhaps there's something more sinister going on here. Work exhausts all of us and leaves little energy for the home. Working in a high-pressure environment, especially in the NHS is hard. You have to suppress so many emotions and predictably, some of these repressed emotions will come out at home. We all recognise this, but we often fail.

## Not your average consultant

I first met Jon after I arrived in the UK in 1990, but his reputation preceded him. I came to the UK specifically to work with him because of his international standing. He was very clever, with a posh English accent, but to his credit insisted that we called him by his first name, which was unusual in those days. He had studied Ancient Greek at one of the Oxbridge colleges, and did very well academically but then decided to go into medicine. Talented young people wanted to work with him because the transplant experience was invaluable and the scientific papers they were given to write would enhance their career.

However, we had to stay late and work hard. I would stay at the hospital until 9:00 pm drafting papers to put on his desk. Unfailingly, my draft would be returned to my desk the next morning, with corrections in red, in his characteristic left-handed scrawl. In terms of getting a paper to a submittable stage, he was the best. He wrote beautiful scientific English and was good at explaining why a paper was novel. It was nice to work in a hospital where papers were accepted by good journals.

Jon kept unusual hours. He seldom arrived at the hospital before 10:00 am but often stayed past midnight. His office was in the same building as his laboratory; he would sit there alone for hours, in the dark. He was eccentric, and to some extent, not of this world. He hardly ever ate breakfast or lunch (he was otherwise occupied) but would then get hungry in the afternoon and would sometimes buy chocolate at the hospital shop. I suppose he must have eaten dinner at some point in the day, but I never saw him do it.

I lead the team of junior doctors who looked after the patients. He trusted us with that, knowing that we would come to him if there were problems. He would do a ward round twice a week, spending quite a brief time in the patients' rooms. Jon cared about the patients and if he was worried, would see them quite late at night. On a ward round, a patient told me that she had a dream that the professor visited her at 2:00 am. "Did he say anything?" I asked.

"No. He just stood in the corner of the room, for about ten minutes. I think he was smiling. I tried to go back to sleep." The patient had severe GVHD and was having a torrid time. I reassured her that he really was there: he wasn't an apparition.

Jon was very wealthy, living in a huge house near the hospital and doing medicine as a hobby (he didn't need the money). He would ask us to present papers at various European conferences but completely forget that poorly paid registrars don't have the wherewithal to fund travel and accommodation. It was a very good experience to present talks to these conferences but sometimes the money had to come out of our pockets, even though Jon had grant income he could have used.

Jon wasn't very good at breaking bad news to patients, partly because he came from an era where prognosis was not always frankly discussed with patients. I remember a round in which we saw a man with unresponsive GVHD, who was in the early stages of dying. Jon said, "Mr Jones, we're reasonably happy with you, but we're not 'completely' happy with you."

One of us stayed behind in the room to 'mop up' and tell the patient what was actually going on. Another time, one of the haematology fellows visited Jon in his office. The weather was terrible and somehow the office ceiling was leaking. Jon was standing on his chair delicately applying correction fluid to the crack in the ceiling. I don't know if it worked. The fellow told this story at his leaving party; there was an embarrassing silence, and no one laughed.

The main advice he gave me was to specialise in one disease: that was the way of becoming well known. It has opened up lots of doors.

Jon received all sorts of honours and gave a number of named lectures. Work was his life. He stayed on in an honorary capacity after he was forced to retire; they found him a desk to work from. He continued to go to conferences to the end.

Oxford. Paddington townhouse. Reserved. Posh voice. Irregular hours. Forgets to eat. Belgian chocolate. Late nights. Eye for the ladies. Open-necked blue shirt. First names used. Dry humour. Ancient Greek. Left-handed scrawl.


## The American boss

Similar to many of my contemporaries, it was always my plan to work in America. In my mid-thirties, I was in no hurry to get a permanent job. I wanted a broader research and transplant experience so that I would be competitive for the best jobs. I had done a year of postdoctoral research in the London lab and was looking for a job that balanced clinical work with research. However, I wasn't really an independent investigator; I wasn't yet experienced enough to lead my own lab program. At the same time, I had a friend in London who was also applying for transplant jobs in the US: his experiences are different to mine but nonetheless instructive.

After multiple application letters to about ten major US cities, Joe (not his real name) was invited to visit about a dozen institutions that had major transplant units, including Dana Farber in Boston, Memorial Sloan Kettering in New York and Stanford in California. Joe decided to work in a major West Coast city hospital with a new transplant unit. The head of the unit was a Jewish American, with a name suggesting Eastern European origins, short and stocky, with thinning grey hair.

A salary of $80,000 US was proposed: Joe accepted. Coming from the NHS that seemed adequate, but he felt in retrospect he could have negotiated something better. More importantly, it gave his boss Dr Rogers (not his real name) the upper hand; even the enlightened President Barack Obama said that money and salaries were the way Americans 'keep score'.

The standard of medicine was good at Joe's hospital, but everybody was under the thumb of the boss. One particular senior oncologist, Conaire, would arrive for an on-call ward round in the transplant unit and say in a rasping, deep, smoke-affected voice, "I hate this fucking place."

Eventually, the transplant unit staff came to see the funny side of this, and clearly venting made him feel better. Rogers, too, was full of contradictions. When Joe initially visited the unit, he drove to his hotel to take him out for dinner. He picked Joe and his wife up at 5:00 pm because he said he was hungry and wanted to get home early and go to bed.

After arriving at the restaurant, Rogers' wife said, "You only need to order your 'entrée' [the main course in America]: we have pre-ordered a starter of New Jersey tomatoes for everybody. They are a speciality here and are flown in fresh from the East Coast."

This turned out to be slices of freshly grown beef tomatoes, with salt and extra virgin olive oil: absolutely delicious. His wife was a well-dressed, socially adept lady from one of the posher suburbs of the town. She was the more intelligent of the two, having been educated at Smith College, a fashionable liberal arts college in Massachusetts. Her role seemed to be to modify her husband's more extreme behaviour, which at times could be outrageous.

Rogers had a lot of unjustified or barely justified opinions. People would ring him for advice, and he would stand on the phone in the middle of the department's office and loudly express his views, presumably for the benefit of everyone in earshot. The secretaries and administrators weren't in the least bit impressed and some of the subject matter was definitely not for public consumption.

One morning, Joe walked into the administrative offices and couldn't help but overhear a member of staff saying, "Hello, Dr Rogers. It's Dr Sparetime on the phone with an urgent referral. Where would you like to take the call?"

"Right here will be fine." Rogers grabbed the phone and spoke loudly. "Hi, Dave, it's Richard Rogers here. I hear you have a new young leukaemic patient. Tell me about her."

Everybody in the office, including visitors, could hear her name, the details of her disease and her social situation. He listened for a while and then interrupted. "She needs a transplant. She shouldn't be managed in Los Altos," he bellowed derisively. "Of course, we'll need to check her insurance status before transferring her."

He was rude to the referring physician and lacked all subtlety. Rogers was hard to like. The more junior faculty also took their referrals in the middle of the office reception area; presumably, they were instructed to do this as a way of emphasising how busy and important they were.

Rogers had a variety of nicknames, many of them unprintable. The fellows hated and feared him to a man (and they were all men). When Joe started work in the unit, he was full of good wishes and positivity. Initially, he defended him against criticism, but not for long. At a meeting of the faculty and middle-grade doctors, one of the smaller fellows dared to express a different opinion on a matter of practice and Rogers became enraged, picked up a chair and threw it at him (fortunately, a somewhat larger fellow caught it, a good thing for both the smaller fellow and the chair).

Such was Rogers's dominance that nobody reported this. Perhaps it was the way they expected a nasty head of department to behave: if you crossed him, you would suffer the consequences.

Although he was a clinician, Rogers ran a research lab. To his credit, it was funded mainly from his private practice, not from conventional external funding sources. He had a particular interest in viruses and other infectious pathogens; he believed they were involved in the pathogenesis of blood cancers. The research in the lab was respectable but received little peer-review funding. Tragically, Jim, the scientific head of the lab died in a car crash six months after Joe arrived. His graduate students were left unsupervised but were still expected to write abstracts and papers and apply for grants.

One of them was Dan. He didn't believe in authority and hated Rogers with a passion. His nickname was 'Regroup man' because when an experiment or idea failed, he always said they needed to 'regroup'. One summer, on the submission deadline day, everyone was asked to read an abstract being sent to the American Society of Haematology. The abstract was logical and well-written; most of the co-authors in the lab read it without suggesting revisions (including Rogers!).

Joe read it carefully. It contained good data; he felt sure it would be accepted. However, he was in for a surprise. The final sentence in the Conclusions section read: 'Rogers gives good head.' Clearly, Dan was testing his colleagues, to see how thoroughly they read the abstract. It was so lucky Joe noticed it; otherwise, it would have gone out and been published. Of course, it was funny, but Dan was admonished for taking such an appalling risk.

In April 1994, Joe travelled overnight to the UK to present a paper at the British Society of Haematology annual meeting and took a day's leave to acclimatise to the time zone. It was a twelve-hour flight to London. When he got back, there was a note under his office door requesting that he come and see Rogers in his office. Joe knocked on his door and said, "Hello."

He didn't say 'welcome back', and he was not smiling. "I know what you did. You added a day to the professional leave. Don't think it went unnoticed."

Joe protested that he was unable to sleep on planes, it was an eight-hour time difference and, that he needed to be rested to give the presentation, but to no avail. Joe had worked very hard in the ward and the lab, but Rogers was horrible, cruelly exerting his power. He was a bully; it reminded Joe of some of his encounters at a private school near London. Joe had no comeback and had to apologise, repeatedly. In those days, in the United States, you could just be fired, for no particular reason.

Rogers was not, however, made of steel. One day, six months after Joe started, he went to the bathroom and was dismayed to see that the toilet was full of blood, followed by severe rectal pain. He had a sigmoidoscopy twenty minutes later (they were scared of him everywhere in the hospital), showing a large cancer of the rectum. He went to a surgeon in Seattle and had it removed. I think he didn't trust the surgeons at his own hospital, possibly because he had been so unpleasant to many of them over the years.

Joe was sympathetic, but not all were. One of the fellows called Joe aside and said, "Don't waste your time worrying about Ricky. He's way too nasty to be killed by bowel cancer."

He was right: Rogers lived another ten years, before dying of something else. There was a positive side to his illness, however: while he was recuperating, Joe and his wife got access to his season tickets at the opera in San Francisco and to some local National Hockey League games of the San Francisco Bulls. Rogers was quite a cultured man. His seats at the opera were dead centre, eight rows back. The opera was an opportunity for an ostentatious display of wealth, but San Franciscans didn't look at it that way.

Being rich was a goal in America and if you achieved it, you let people know. Joe and his wife were among the few not wearing fur coats. Apart from his boss, Joe regards his time on the West Coast as important in his career development. My experiences were also positive, but I worked in Philadelphia. Joe and I met up frequently in the US to compare our experiences over a couple of beers.

Philadelphia is a historic city with preserved architecture from the late eighteenth century, good restaurants and a lively art and music culture. We bought an old house in Society Hill, walking distance from the hospital, and stayed in the US for three years, did quite a lot of travelling and made some long-term friends. I also got to know my transplant and leukaemia counterparts in America; that has been a big advantage throughout my career. My wife got a faculty job at an Ivy League university hospital, but despite productive clinical and translational research, I never felt comfortable living in the US and wanted to move. I was offered good jobs in New York (and others in other East and West Coast cities), but in 1996, my wife's brother was diagnosed with lymphoma, and we decided to return to the UK.

Nevertheless, there is a lot about American medicine and medical research in the US is second to none. The best medicine is as good as anywhere in the world unless you didn't have medical insurance. I remember asking my colleagues what happened to poor people with leukaemia who needed a transplant, and they said they didn't know. More disturbingly, it didn't seem to worry them. It was a good experience to live and work there, but medicine was too money driven for my tastes.

I was idealistic and didn't like medicine being regarded as a profit-making business. However, in 1993, big American hospitals had an electronic prescribing system, using the primitive computers available then, so they could charge money for drugs accurately. In the US, twenty-seven years ago, they could tell us exactly how much of each drug was prescribed. In spite of the much-vaunted 'digital NHS', we still cannot do that in my hospital in the UK, in 2022.

## The good doctor

Although her patients always called her Dr Brown out of respect, Penny (not her real name) certainly wouldn't think she was worth writing about. She was middle-class, from a city well away from London. She won a scholarship to an excellent school that had a record of getting its pupils into good universities. During her final year at school, she decided to be a doctor but didn't get into medicine initially; she had to be interviewed for the few remaining places.

She was good at interviews and knew exactly what was required (the 'right' answers). She got into medical school and after five years of study and ten years of training in medicine and haematology, she applied for a consultant post, having worked at the best haematology units in London and become highly regarded as a broadly trained haematologist.

She did a period of laboratory research and gained a research degree. Although this was very competently done, research wasn't her long-term goal: she wanted to look after patients. Talking to patients, reassuring them and explaining what lay ahead, and offering patients clinical trials so that they could receive state-of-the-art therapy was her strength.

Penny always seemed to be smiling; that was her default facial expression. She projected warmth and a steadiness that patients liked. They knew she cared about them, and she always did her best for them, feeling guilty if she didn't do everything she could. She sometimes got cross or frustrated with the NHS but retained her professional demeanour. She was in many ways a product of the NHS and knew its limitations first-hand. She was also a gifted clinician manager who made an effort to understand the issues and had a reputation for being fair.

The non-medical managers loved working with her because she got things done. If a job plan needed to be written, she wouldn't wait till somebody else did it but do it herself. Penny specialised in a particular blood cancer and over her thirty-year consultant career saw it change from an incurable disease with an average survival of five years to a chronic disease where many patients survived more than ten years, and some were effectively cured. As an attending consultant on the inpatient haematology ward, she was one of the best.

The patients were all seen, every round, no matter how long it took, and she made time to communicate with the patients and their families. The registrar and the junior doctor on the ward had to work hard to meet her standards, but they didn't mind because she led by example. When she referred patients for transplants, her medical assessment of the patient was detailed and accurate, and she was quite the best-referring consultant I had to deal with. The referred patients never had undiagnosed medical issues that affected the decision to transplant.

Penny loved her work, but her family was the priority. She made every effort to prevent her work from impinging on family time although of course that wasn't always possible. She was always available for her children and yet felt guilty when she missed any of her clinical commitments. This was despite her working much longer hours than she was paid for. She was diligent to a fault. There are many doctors like this. You will never know their names.

## The good nurse

Eunice was the tiny charge nurse (a 'sister') of the ward for my first medical registrar job, in my third year after qualification. Eunice was five feet two, thin, with short black hair and an immaculately starched nurse's uniform. She was very good-looking but didn't indulge in flirtation or small talk: she was too focused on running the ward smoothly. She was in her late twenties but already had ten years of experience. There were constant bed pressures, very ill patients and lots of elective admissions every week; I knew our working relationship would be important. She often stayed for hours after her shift finished (most unusual for nurses nowadays).

Eunice was from Kuala Lumpur and ran the medical ward as a benign dictatorship. The consultants trusted her decisions because she was nearly always right. She knew a lot more practical medicine than the interns and knew how to get things done. If a patient needed an urgent scan or a rapid referral, she knew how to go about it. She was one of the best nurses I have ever worked with and repeatedly saved me from errors or omissions.

We had a real bond. I think she liked me because I worked hard and was ambitious. Once, we were alone on the ward at the sister's station at about 7:30 pm. I was sighing with tiredness, and she touched me on the cheek. I turned around and smiled, but nothing happened because a junior nurse arrived, and the moment passed.

## A certain military bearing

Ander had led an unusual life. He was born in the UK, but his family moved to Australia when he was young. For some reason, he would always say he felt British. He went to medical school in Australia but then spent most of his professional life working in the USA.

He got a consultant job in Melbourne but wanted to work in London, as did many Australian doctors. His chance came when a haematologist at one of the great London hospitals was killed by an IRA car bomb while walking in central London. There was suddenly a vacancy at the hospital and Ander was available at short notice. He and his family moved to London.

He was a prolific researcher, very good at writing papers, and good at looking after patients. However, he was not liked; the reasons for this are not clear, but he was certainly different. Consultant appointments in the UK are permanent, but it was clear he would never be a professor. On weekends, he worked with the British territorial army.

All doctors start with the rank of captain, but he had risen to major, and at school, he had been the highest-ranked cadet; his nickname at the hospital was 'the Colonel'. He had a formality, a slight stiffness that many in the army did. He acquired a sort of home county's accent, and there was little of Australia left in him.

In the army, he was popular with the men he commanded, partly because of his ability to drink. He also was able to perform a physical feat that none of his men could, squatting down on either leg with the other outstretched, then rising again. He won a lot of money betting that others couldn't do this. His office at the London hospital was similar to him: old-fashioned and of a different era.

It was not shared and that was a good thing, as it was always full of cigarette smoke; he probably smoked twenty a day in working hours alone. There were pictures of his family on his desk but most prominent were pictures of him in military uniform at various army occasions. A large photo of Winston Churchill was behind his desk (the man he most admired) and a union jack was visible in the corner of the room.

He became an international expert in chronic leukaemia and wrote important reviews in major British journals, but he wanted to be a professor and that required moving to America. His wife and children were well ensconced in the UK; they didn't move with him, and he only saw them on holidays. This was not good for him. He continued to smoke, and drink way too much. Partly because of his position of influence, height (he was six foot, which is tall for his generation) and muscular build, he seemed attractive to women, and once boasted to his sister that he had bedded over a hundred.

In America, you can rise to a full professor based on academic achievement alone; this was no problem for him as he was an author of hundreds of papers. His big break came when he was the first to use a new treatment for rare chronic leukaemia. He published this rapidly and then became the chief investigator for the Eastern Cooperative Oncology Group trial of this drug. This was a positive trial; he became well known and published the data in the *New England Journal of Medicine*, as well as giving major talks at all the big haematology conferences.

His legacy seemed assured until somebody checked the toxicity data: he had underestimated or possibly falsified the side effects of the experimental drug used in the trial. The drug worked, but it was far more toxic than previously reported. ECOG investigated this and expelled him from the organisation, although he always maintained his innocence. He moved to a southern city to work, possibly to escape this criticism; one had the feeling that the end of his career was less fun than the beginning.

When he was sixty-five, his health was declining, so he retired and moved back to the UK, where he was able to buy a huge house overlooking the Thames, in a very sought-after area. He still maintained links with the army and retained the rank of Lieutenant Colonel (retired).


## My PhD 'supervisor'

For an academic doctor training in research, a key relationship is with your PhD supervisor. Doing laboratory research is completely different to looking after patients: you need to be shepherded through the process of deciding on a project, getting a grant, learning how to do experiments, and confronting frustration and failure. The best supervisors are invested in the research project, and staff should only agree to be a supervisor if they have time to carry out all these roles. Often the project forms a part of the supervisor's overall research strategy, including regular lab meetings to track progress. The lab personnel should be a tight-knit team.

My PhD supervisor Robert helped me with the initial grant application to fund the PhD (he had to because I didn't understand what we were going to investigate, mainly because he wasn't patient enough to explain it; it later turned out that he did not understand it himself in any great depth). My topic was 'Mechanisms of cytotoxic drug action' or how anti-cancer drugs kill cancer cells. He called the research 'biochemical pharmacology' and I focused on ADP ribosylation as a mechanism of (cancer) cell death, which may mean little to the non-medical reader.

In hindsight, I should have sought a more highly powered supervisor who was more invested in the research, understood it fully and considered it part of his own research program. Some of my colleagues had spent a year during medical school doing laboratory research projects and knew better how to go about getting a good PhD supervisor and project. These are the things nobody tells you.

We started off measuring various chemicals within cells and then diverged into apoptosis (a form of cell death), which enabled me to learn some basic molecular biology, as all my contemporaries undertaking PhDs were doing. Robert met with me about once a month but never really went through my experiments, many of which didn't work initially (as is common). Of course, I asked for advice, but although there was a very young lab tech who helped a bit (but mainly played computer games), in a bigger lab, there would have been a weekly meeting where the results of experiments were discussed. Without this guidance, I decided on the direction of research and what literature to read, tasks I was barely equipped to undertake.

I am ashamed to say that I used to fantasise about Robert having a car accident. I hated him. He lost (yes, properly lost or discarded) two of my six PhD chapters. He was ridiculously disorganised. Mail, drafts of scientific papers and patient notes were thrown onto his desk, piling up to about a foot above the desk surface.

Every so often, he swept everything into a bin, reasoning that if it was still needed, the person concerned would remind him of it. This was the late 'eighties and was the very beginning of PhD students using word processors, so I had the lost PhD chapters on my desktop, fortunately. However, it caused considerable delay because he didn't know what had happened to them. I had accepted a job in London and needed to submit my PhD before leaving.

"Prof, I wonder if you have had a chance to look at Chapter 4, the chapter on apoptosis?"

"When did you give it to me?"

"About two weeks ago. I put it on your desk with a note."

"I had to clear my desk. Can you give it to me again?"

"Sure. I'll also give you Chapter 5 again." He had put that in the bin, too.

My PhD is around two hundred pages; each chapter was about twenty-five pages of printed material, with figures and tables showing the results. Supervisors generally look at each PhD chapter in detail once, and then it's up to the candidate to revise it until there is a final version. He seemed more interested in publications than the thesis itself, and we did get a paper in the Journal of Clinical Investigation, which is a good journal; I wrote the paper, and he edited several drafts. This high-impact paper helped me get my next job.

At the end of the PhD, he invited me over for dinner, but I think his wife was away and nothing was prepared when I arrived at his house. He served me three reheated, lukewarm rissoles, one of which had a bite out of it (he was hungry). Right through the three years of research, I tried to make appointments to discuss my data and where to go next, but he didn't know where he would be at any point in time and didn't keep a diary. I would track him down in his office to agree on some general goals (I had given up on specific advice), but after a few minutes he would get bored and say he had to 'go to a meeting'.

He had the attention span of a toddler; if I had died, he would have scarcely noticed. I know from my own experience subsequently that having a PhD student is a huge responsibility: you are responsible for getting their work over the finishing line, no matter what happens. It's much more regulated now: universities require regular progress reports from candidates and supervisors, and supervisors have to be involved in the students' pastoral care.

The submitted PhD is sent off to two examiners, chosen by the supervisor. One of the assessors of my PhD didn't respond to reminders from the university to submit his comments, and Robert didn't chase him up. In the meantime, I moved to the UK and had to contact him from there to get him to do this. Eventually, I found out that the marker (who was a former colleague of Robert's) had suffered a heart attack, and my PhD had to be reassigned. Robert literally didn't give a shit and didn't even congratulate me when I was awarded the degree.

Fortunately, only minor revisions were required, which fitted on a single A4 page and took less than half an hour to do. If more major revisions had been required, there is no way he could have helped. I got four first-authored papers out of it the PhD, including one in a top-flight journal. I could do the technical stuff in the lab, and I could plan and interpret experiments, but I didn't love the work. However, it taught me how to look at scientific literature more critically and to understand scientific advances in ALL and transplants. I recommend it to all haematologists wanting to work in an academic teaching hospital.

## Tony

Tony wouldn't want me to make a fuss. I applied for a job in Bristol in 1996 because it was home to the first BMT unit in the UK to successfully use unrelated donors as a source of stem cells. Only a quarter of patients needing a transplant have a matched sibling donor and need an alternative stem cell source. In 2022, nearly 60% of transplants use unrelated donors from one of the worldwide registries.

Tony, a paediatric oncologist, decided he would do these transplants and found a way of overcoming the problems and didn't really allow anybody to get in the way, an attitude that appealed to me. Plan it carefully, then just do it. He was physically large and solid, but there was also a gentleness there.

Tony had a particular way of dealing with his patients, deciding how ill they were by whether they laughed at his jokes. On his way into the room, he would bump his head into the door, pretend it had really hurt him, and then, if that didn't elicit a laugh, sneeze and wipe his nose on his tie, which was invariably bright with animals or cartoon characters on it. I found this quite annoying and wondered if it worked. He had a long career, he was one of the few consultants I have met who couldn't drive, even though he mainly lived outside Bristol and had to take a taxi into the hospital every day and when he was on call.

Outside medicine, Tony was a highly intelligent, cultured man who loved literature and classical music. At his funeral, which he planned, he included a number of classical musical pieces, many of which I now associate with his demise. He was a very private man, so when he became ill, we knew very little about it. He had sarcoma of the lung and didn't respond to chemotherapy. He was palliated at home and was looked after by his wife, also a doctor.

When he died, we all assembled at a beautiful old church in the Somerset countryside, all very English. The sky was a bright blue but there were clouds.

Tony had prepared a speech, which was read to us, thanking all the people who had looked after him, particularly his wife. His best friend gave a candid assessment of him, describing him as an intellectual, who loved rugby but who also could be 'shirty'. There was definitely a darker, more brooding side to him, possibly related to seeing all those children with leukaemia die.

We all listened to 'The lark ascending' for fifteen minutes in sadness. He had done some fantastic things (including curing lots of children) but life didn't always seem to make him happy. One possible exception to this was when England won the rugby World Cup against Australia. He cornered me before the game and said, "I'm very sorry, but England are going to win this."

I agreed. When England won narrowly, he had a look of smug satisfaction; he would have been so grumpy if they had lost.

## How groups function: Covering the weekend

Eleven haematology consultants joined the scheduled Webex call. The consultant on call for the weekend was self-isolating because his son had tested positive for COVID. His son had caught the virus from schoolmates and was absolutely fine, wanting to go and play rugby. Another colleague was ill with a cough and other minor viral symptoms and was waiting for a COVID PCR result: she couldn't come to work. That left nine people.

Somebody had to cover the weekend but nobody wanted to do it. They were not in a good mood; they were tired and didn't want to give up their weekend plans. It would mean telling their long-suffering spouse that they had to look after the kids and that they wouldn't get much help.

I was flying on Friday evening to Mallorca so I couldn't do it. Others said things like: 'I have to go to Hereford on Sunday' or 'I have been attending for three of the last four weeks, I need a break'. Nobody was remotely interested in the social plans of their colleagues (or how tired they were) and wanted them to ditch the plans, and (just) cover the weekend.

There was a grudging acceptance that they would 'muck in' and share it out. Everybody sounded depressed: nobody was smiling. There was an official second-on-call rota, but it hadn't worked. All of the winter lay ahead, and a soup of viruses awaited us.

As infection lead, I had done a lot of work to get consultants tested for the non-COVID viruses but this was proving difficult. We couldn't decide where the swabs would be done, where they would be processed and how they would be paid for. I passed the financial issue onto the managers—this was not my remit. Every viral infection meant missing work.

## The National CAR-T-cell therapy panel

I have evaluated and criticised lots of organisations, particularly the NHS and mainly for the way it is run. However, there are bright spots. For example, it would be remiss of me to not mention some fantastic colleagues. when CAR-T-cell therapy started in the UK, it was heavily regulated by NHS England, not always in a helpful way. They made us meet to discuss every patient, as a way of controlling costs.

The therapy costs up to half a million pounds per patient and the clinical decisions are complex. We typically discuss three or four patients every fortnight and each one gets no more than fifteen minutes. After two years, we were told they no longer required us to meet to discuss patients, but we decided to continue the meeting for the benefit of patients with ALL. This panel has no funding, and the chairs commonly send out minutes late in the evening.

We meet every two weeks. There are three chairs: Sara, Persis and Rachael, each of them outstanding. The panel consists of the lead in ALL at each of the six CAR-T-cell centres and all are experts (I represent Bristol). Everybody listens to each other: the chairs get the best out of the panel. It is well-organised, and we have all the patient details.

We have published our results, which are also outstanding, showing that 60% of the patients we treat are alive and without leukaemia a year after receiving CAR T-cells. These results are better than the results of the trial that proved that this therapy worked. The opinions from the panel are world-class; there is intellectual flexibility and a willingness to learn. It is both serious and light-hearted. We discuss children and young adults with treatment-resistant ALL who would die without this therapy, but also tell jokes and ask after each other.

We seek advice about other patients. We are friends. This is the best clinical meeting I attend. One of the chairs said, "I love it. I learn so much." My Australian CAR-T-cell fellow listens in and once said the discussion was so good that she wanted to record it. Can the NHS take credit for this? Not really, even though all of us work for it. This work is extra. We do it for nothing, to make sure our patients get the best.

# Chapter 5
# Being a Patient

Despite all our experience, it's not possible for haematologists to know fully what it's like to have acute leukaemia, to be really ill and scared that if things don't go according to plan you will rapidly die. Nevertheless, I do have some insight through my own experiences with ill health but also from my first-hand conversations with patients and their families facing huge changes in their lives, and possibly death. The way we cope with these challenges is the measure of us as people: it reflects our personality and our strength. And of course, some people can't cope with the situations presented by this diagnosis. They deserve our help.

To be a good doctor you need to be able to put yourself in the position of the patient. What are they thinking? What are their main concerns? How can you alleviate their anxiety? What's it like to have blood cancer and have your whole life turned upside down? This chapter will tell more patient stories but this time they are from a personal perspective, including the story of two doctors with blood cancer. One of them is me.

## My family: An excess of myeloma

About fifteen years ago, Andrew, the second-oldest of my four brothers, was incidentally found to have an abnormal protein in his blood. It is called a paraprotein, a common finding as people age. The protein is made by plasma cells, a type of white blood cell in the bone marrow that makes the antibodies we need to fight infections. This condition is called MGUS[2], and although it is not cancer, it is regarded as premalignant (i.e. it may precede cancer). Initially, this

---

[2] MGUS is a monoclonal gammopathy of uncertain significance. For some, this is a relatively benign problem, and in others, it progresses to myeloma, a largely incurable disease.

was just something for his doctor to keep an eye on, but over time the amount of this paraprotein slowly grew, and in 2015 he met the criteria for a diagnosis of myeloma.

Andrew's blood problem, which had been a worrying inconvenience requiring twice-yearly blood tests, became a malignancy that required treatment. My brother, who worked as a lawyer, has always had a good understanding of his health problems. These days, he even reads scientific papers about trials of treatment for myeloma and made sure he was being looked after by a very good myeloma doctor. This transformation to a cancer came as no surprise, but it was life-changing for him. He knows he will one day probably die of this disease and wants to do everything he can to stay alive.

Myeloma is a specific type of bone marrow cancer arising from plasma cells, a different kind of white cell to those affected by leukaemia, found mainly in the bone marrow and seldom in the blood. It is not leukaemia. The malignant plasma cells grow too rapidly, occupying the bone marrow, often causing anaemia and damaging the bones and kidneys. Very few patients with myeloma are cured. Out of hundreds of myeloma patients I have looked after, only ten of those patients are considered cured.

For most people, treatment extends their lives, with patients living an average of around seven years after diagnosis. The great majority of younger patients get a disease response to treatment; many have a stem cell transplant and enjoy good periods of survival, often with a quality of life that is normal or close to normal. However, some have more aggressive diseases, with severe bony involvement, causing pain, debility and a greatly reduced quality of life.

In early 2016, three months after Andrew's diagnosis, my younger brother Michael was also diagnosed with myeloma. He also knew he had an abnormal protein in his blood, which he had chosen not to tell us about. This increased and a bone marrow biopsy showed 'smouldering' (early) myeloma.

He is a paediatrician and out of the blue called to say that he had a 'touch' of myeloma (cancer). I think this was an attempt at humour: all of us were shocked. We managed to help him to get onto a trial of a new antibody (daratumumab) directed against plasma cells. He had to restrict his fluid intake to make the paraprotein level more than ten grams per litre in order to meet the eligibility criteria for the three-year trial.

Is having two brothers with myeloma just bad luck? Not exactly. Myeloma does have an increased incidence in families but having two siblings with myeloma is very unusual. It's so unusual that when I tell colleagues, they sometimes think I am mistaken. Myeloma is a rare cancer, so my increased relative risk of myeloma didn't really worry me, and indeed none of the rest of the family currently have myeloma (we were all tested). I should mention that my wife Jenny is a nationally known myeloma doctor, which has been very useful for my brothers.

She is close to them, and they trust her opinion absolutely. Jenny and I explained things to my brothers and reassured them where possible but mostly looked on in disbelief as their lives were irrevocably altered. Michael, who was fifty-five at diagnosis, initially seemed to carry on as if nothing had happened. He had his antibody treatment every eight weeks and continued to work full-time as a paediatrician, although he no longer looks after acutely ill children to reduce his chance of getting infections, and he has monthly immunoglobulin treatment. He didn't really respond to the trial treatment (his paraprotein level remained the same), but his myeloma did not progress either, so he probably benefitted from the trial.

Sometime later after the trial came to an end, the drug company offered those who took part the opportunity to restart the treatment (a very expensive drug), at no charge. Michael accepted this offer and remains well. However, the drug will not be free indefinitely and Michael will have a difficult decision to make: self-funding the drug would be hard.

Andrew, who was sixty at diagnosis, had 'active' myeloma. He needed treatment because it threatened his bones and kidney function. His initial treatment only worked to an extent, barely halving his paraprotein levels (a partial response). He then had an autologous stem cell transplant, which again only worked in part. Andrew went out to dinner every night for seven nights before being admitted to the hospital for the transplant.

Unfortunately, he caught two viruses, which made him ill for ten weeks, although not life-threateningly. Nevertheless, this turned a normally simple procedure into something quite unpleasant. His myeloma relapsed nine months after the transplant, putting him into a poor prognostic group with an average survival of less than two years. Andrew had read about this and knew how bad things looked. That's when my wife and I became useful. We suggested he enquire about a new three-drug regimen (lenalidomide, daratumumab and dexamethasone), including the antibody that Michael had received as part of the trial.

His consultant agreed, and although he has had to pay a great deal of money for this treatment, it has worked. It put him into a deep remission and has kept him there for over three years. He is now more than five years from diagnosis, a milestone none of us thought he would reach. Of course, most people in Australia or the UK would not have access to this treatment, which is routinely available in the USA. Andrew needs the drugs to stay alive, and of course, it isn't his fault that other patients can't obtain them, but for cancer doctors, there are complex and common ethical issues around patients having unequal access to drugs. I felt relieved that he had received the best treatment, but of course, it is unfair that not everybody gets the best therapy.

Both Michael and Andrew had a difficult time with COVID because we couldn't be sure they would respond to the vaccines. Andrew didn't leave home much and hardly saw anybody. This was not good for him, and worst of all, he didn't feel safe travelling. In fact, he was tested, and he has made antibodies in response to the vaccine, suggesting he is at least partially protected. Michael has only recently resumed travelling and that was after receiving Evusheld, a two-antibody infusion against the virus, and having access to Paxlovid.

I have learnt a lot from this, both about what it means to be ill and what it means to be powerless. Of course, it also made me closer to my brothers. Unusually (for me), I decided to do something positive. I got on my bike and rode with my wife from London to Paris on a group ride organised by the charity Myeloma UK.

We raised £6,000 for myeloma research, but mainly I did it to show my brothers that I cared about them, their families and their struggle to survive. Five years later, I did the ride again and raised more money. However, at some point, the myeloma will come back and that's when things may become more difficult, both medically and emotionally, for all of us.

### Ten out of ten pain

The presentation was classic. I was twenty-four, midway through my third year as a doctor at the Royal Melbourne Hospital and was doing the prestigious renal rotation with the world-famous nephrologist Professor Priscilla Kincaid-Smith. I had just come back from a holiday in Eastern Europe and had drunk very little on some days because of the risk of getting giardia from tap water in St Petersburg and Moscow (bottled water was not easily available). I got home late, quickly ate my dinner then went off to bed. I woke in the middle of the night.

It had been a long day, finishing at 8:00 pm with very little time to eat or drink. Nowadays, junior doctors have mandatory meal breaks and carry water with them. A pain in my left side was easing off. What could it be? Five minutes later, the pain was back, the worst pain I have ever had, in colicky waves. I could also feel some pain in my testicle, which I recognised as referred pain. (When you have pain in one part of the body, you can experience pain in other places supplied by the same nerves.)

*Bloody hell, I've got renal colic!* I thought. The pain was so ridiculously bad I started laughing. I didn't have any painkiller tablets that would remotely help with this intensity of pain: I needed opiates.

Doctors often ask patients to describe the pain they are experiencing. I would have found it very hard to describe this terrible pain. There was a sharpness to it, and it came and went. We rank pain severity out of ten: this was definitely ten out of ten.

I was driven to the front of the hospital, then entered the A&E department where I was well-known, walked straight through the triage area past a nurse I recognised, saying, "I think I've got renal colic. Can I have a bottle to wee in?"

I was ghostly pale and soon doubled over in pain: there wasn't much doubt about the diagnosis. I had been admitting officer in the A&E the previous year, so they knew I could make quick, accurate diagnoses, apparently including for myself. "Can I use cubicle five, please?"

I passed urine into the bottle. My urine was bright red, the colour of blood. The diagnosis was made.

"Can I have some pain relief, please?" I asked a busy passing nurse.

"Yep, David, just getting a doctor to write it up." She looked hassled but soon arrived with a butterfly needle, which she skilfully inserted, followed by 150mg of intravenous pethidine. I could feel the pain subside, I started to relax and stopped caring about the pain. I felt sleepy and sank back into the narrow bed in the cubicle. In the A&E, they imaged my urinary tract with intravenous iodine.

I was allergic to this and developed an itchy red rash all over that needed an antihistamine. It was not my day. A hospital porter took me up to the renal ward, past several nurses and doctors I worked with. The junior doctor I was working with, Sally, said: "Hi David, I'm afraid I will have to admit you. It'll be quick."

"Don't be embarrassed Sally, I am past caring."

She took a brief history and examined my abdomen. My tummy wasn't sore but examining me made her blush.

"I think you know what we are going to do. You will need more pain relief and fluids, and hopefully, the stone will pass. If it does, it would be worth sending it off to see what type it is." The X-ray had shown a small stone in my left ureter. "We should be able to discharge you tomorrow. Your kidney function is excellent. I hope you get some sleep."

My consultant came to see me in the morning, without the trailing medical students. "Has the pain gone?" he asked.

I nodded. "We'll do some tests to work out why you got this stone, but you need to drink more. Have the rest of the day off but probably you'll be OK to return to work tomorrow."

He was right: I was absolutely fine the next day.

This was the first of many kidney stone episodes. Not drinking enough while working and having holidays where there was poor access to hydration had undoubtedly contributed. It's very hard to change habits, but I've tried. One urologist told me that when I got up at night to pass urine, I should drink a pint of water! If I did that, I would spend the whole night in the loo. He meant well, but it wasn't good advice.

I still can't describe how bad the pain of renal colic is. It is so bad you can't believe it. You go white in the face; you feel faint and nauseated; you grit your teeth and just hope it will pass. Having severe pain like this has helped me understand what my leukaemia patients go through when they have severe bone pain.

### Life change—being diagnosed

On Guy Fawkes Day in 2021, I was diagnosed with small lymphocytic lymphoma, which is essentially the same disease as chronic lymphocytic leukaemia (CLL), the most common leukaemia in adults. In September and October, I had been worried about persistently enlarged lymph nodes in my neck and armpits, but I thought it might have been due to the COVID booster I had in late September (I had had an extreme reaction to the vaccine, with massive swelling in my left shoulder, the deltoid muscle), but there were too many lymph nodes, and they weren't on the same side as the booster. I had looked it up in the literature and it was possible, but it became harder to justify.

I finally stopped making excuses and plucked up the courage to see my colleague, who sent me off for an ultrasound of the neck lumps. It took two days to get the appointment. I waited outside to be called, I had been worrying about this. My wife was in Cornwall on a pre-arranged trip; we somehow had not allowed ourselves to admit this possibility. I sat on the examination couch while she looked at the neck lumps on her scanner. "They're not normal," she said, without making eye contact. She had diagnosed a lot of cancers in doctors.

"Is the hilum obliterated?" I asked. She nodded. "Do they look malignant?"

"Yes, I am afraid so."

"Do you think it is lymphoma?"

"Yes, or CLL/SLL."

"If it was anybody else, we would do a biopsy."

"Let's go ahead." She took a liquid sample from a node for flow and three biopsies. It didn't hurt. "Do you want me to organise a CT scan now, while you are here?"

"Yes, please. Can I ask a favour, can you report it and tell me what it shows?"

"No problem, I'll do it when I finish this clinic."

I rang Jenny from the examination couch. "Jenny it's bad news, it's almost certainly lymphoma, the nodes are not reactive."

She said she would come home immediately. Even the CT scan wasn't easy: four attempts to get into a vein, in a very cold room, more bruises. They had to cannulate a vein in my leg.

Once the contrast was in, the scan was quick. The radiologist rang me with the results and then sent me photos for my records. So many more nodes than I thought, and bigger. It was unpleasant to look at, but I needed to see it. But I needed to see it.

I contacted the lymphoma consultant who was off that day. She wouldn't be back until Monday, and I couldn't wait. 'Laura, it's lymphoma.' She sent a message 'Goodness.' She had been rung about the scan, it was stage 3. She knew I had no symptoms and was really well.

After all that, I walked home to wait for some early results. (Later Laura called me to tell me it was CLL, one of the most indolent lymphomas.) I had bought a sandwich but wasn't in the least bit interested in eating it. The slightly late diagnosis didn't matter, and it was better to have it resolved.

I didn't cry until I told the kids. They reacted in different ways but obviously understood everything. I shall never forget telling Thomas on a FaceTime call. He covered his eyes and cried. Thomas is a vet.

He had looked after dogs and cats with lymphoma, and although they responded to treatment, they all died. This is different to humans, I explained—it is one of the most treatable cancers. I told him that I hoped to do well but that this was a life-altering event and it would mean I might not be there for Mummy in her old age, and for them in their middle age. I asked him if he had any questions, and he said he had none and would try to take it on board and get used to it. We said we would come and see him later in the week, and we would talk more then. He said he would try to not think about it all the time because it made him upset.

However, Thomas had been ill with a virus, and unfortunately, I caught it when I saw him. This necessitated two weeks of steroids, codeine, puffers and two GP consultations. It made me miserable and quite unable to deal with the diagnosis. I was awake at night and taking a lot of drugs, which made me feel depressed.

This was the worst time in my life. Everything had changed. My coping mechanism was to read everything I could about it, and I went to see a world expert in Oxford, who spoke to me and Jenny for an hour and a half. He will be there when we have to make a treatment decision. (The data is constantly evolving; there are several ongoing trials of new therapies.) The median time to need treatment in my type of CLL is three years, but it can be much longer.

I am now the third person in my family to receive a blood cancer diagnosis, and my oldest brother has had localised thyroid cancer that is considered cured. Is my diagnosis related to theirs? We don't really know, but CLL is different to myeloma. We saw a clinical genetics consultant but there were no relevant tests to do that would prove or disprove the possible link. For a family with six children, cancer diagnoses in four of them are not much more than one would expect.

## The anxieties of waiting

When you are a cancer patient waiting is probably the single worst part of the experience. I also believe it is the main reason that cancer outcomes in the UK are not as good as comparable, neighbouring countries. We should all be in more of a hurry.

When an abnormality is found on an X-ray that raises the possibility of cancer, it commonly takes weeks for that change to be reported and communicated. Then there is usually a biopsy that makes the diagnosis. Another wait to get the biopsy done.

For that biopsy to be reported and then discussed in an MDT, commonly takes two weeks. At that point, treatment is mandated to start within sixty-two days, or this is considered a breach. Hospitals are worried about breaches because meeting government targets is one of the ways they are assessed. Where did sixty-two days come from? Cancer can spread or worsen at that time.

Let's look at it from the patient's point of view. From initial diagnostic test(s), through definitive biopsies, histology, MDT and multiple delays it can take three months. This causes anxiety per se, patients can't function while their mind is elsewhere. As if the cancer itself wasn't enough to worry about. Does it have to be this way? Absolutely not.

A patient with leukaemia or high-grade lymphoma can progress from initial diagnosis to treatment in two to five days and sometimes we have to start treatment on the day they arrive at the hospital. To shorten waiting times we need more resources and more people at every stage of the process, more scanners, more radiologists, pathologists but most of all, a different attitude. Put simply, to cure more patients with cancer, we need to spend more money.

## Six-month review

When you have cancer, waiting for results is the hardest bit. Throughout my holiday, I knew I was going to have a scan and repeat blood tests. The day finally came. The blood test was better: my platelets had come up to normal and my white cell count was up a bit. As usual, it was hard to find a vein. It blew in the CT scanner, and I had to arrange another line.

Finally, the scan itself only took a few minutes. I had asked for the scan to be reported by Mandy, the radiologist who made the diagnosis. I didn't want to nag her, but I also couldn't wait any longer. I couldn't think about anything else: it was driving me crazy. She emailed me to tell me that the nodes were a bit bigger but overall it was considered stable disease, meaning that I would remain off therapy, being observed.

I realise I will need treatment someday because it will continue to grow, hopefully slowly. My next appointment is in about four months, roughly one year from diagnosis. I will try to put it to the back of my mind, which is not easy for me. I am training for a charity bike ride from London to Paris—this is a good distraction and helps reinforce that I am well.

## One-year review

On Guy Fawkes Day 2022, I reached one year from my formal diagnosis (even though my symptoms preceded that date). No celebration, no explosions. I'm not going to make too much of this, it's not really the main subject matter of the book. It gives me a personal insight into what my patients go through, although my disease is far more chronic.

At a recent review by my consultant, the lymph nodes were not significantly larger, but my lymphocyte count had risen from five to seven (a 40% rise) over five and a half months. I remain well, with no clear symptoms and my successful London to Paris bike ride argues against any significant progression. It was nice to be told I don't need to be seen for six months.

Although I think about my CLL every day, I try to 'park' it. The average time to needing treatment is three years, but it could be sooner than that, or longer. This is my personal struggle. It is a nervous time as I approach every review and not easy for my family.

## Coping with being in the hospital

I have spent forty years working in hospitals: I am used to the environment, which no longer seems strange. Most of the patients I see are in hospital beds in single rooms. It's worth considering what it's like to be a patient, lying on a bed looking up at your doctor. I think I have been admitted to the hospital on maybe a dozen occasions, but never for more than a few days. When our son was two and had complicated appendicitis, he was in the hospital for two weeks, with one of us always by the bedside.

It's never pleasant: hospital rooms are not comfortable places. There's not enough space and the chairs round the bed are not designed for visitors to spend a prolonged time in. There's no privacy—people are constantly looking through the glass window in the door, or coming in to adjust an intravenous drip, deliver medication or offer a cup of tea, and yet despite all these people entering the room, it feels lonely and strange.

It's even harder when the stay is prolonged. What is it like to have a bone marrow transplant, and be in hospital for several weeks? It's hard to imagine how dehumanising it can be. Some patients and their families try to make the hospital room similar to their home. As an example, I will describe a recent patient's room.

Roger had a big room, one of those we reserve for long-stay patients, spacious with large windows that gave city views, but very little room for visitors to sit or stand. There was an exercise bike at one end of the room and a small sofa at the other. I found a chair, which I pulled up to the side of the bed. On the wall facing the bed were photos of Roger's wife and children. To the left were carefully arranged rows of cards from various well-wishers, family and friends, in all shapes and sizes, some quite garish.

There were two 'Get well!' balloons tied to the end of the bed, both bright red. His bed tray was crammed with biscuits, chocolate, baby oranges and other fruit. There was only just enough space for the obligatory plastic water jug and cup. The sofa held his laptop, his mobile, the chargers, and, strangely, a child's iPad (children weren't allowed to visit). Roger even had his own duvet and pillowcases, in a tasteful light grey.

He saw me looking at the ridiculous amount of brought-in food and asked me if I was hungry. I explained that we weren't allowed to eat the patients' food, and more to the point, I wanted him to eat it. The room was full and untidy to the point of making me feel uncomfortable, but he had made it his home, as far away from a hospital room as one could imagine.

Of course, there's much more a hospital patient can do, using technology, to normalise being in the hospital. WhatsApp, FaceTime and other video technologies enable real-time visual contact with family and friends. One man kept his phone on at night so he could see and hear his partner during the night as if he was sleeping with her. Before the pandemic, many patients were able to have a partner or parent sleep on a fold-away bed in the room. Just having a familiar person in the room helps, even if they don't talk much.

## The relative unimportance of being Earnest

Ernie, my father-in-law was an increasingly frail ninety-two-year-old man, who was having a year of poor health. He had played tennis until his late eighties but had to retire from the sport because of hip and back problems. A few months back, he had broken his hip tripping over his walker on the way to the bathroom. As the ambulance men carried him out, he said to his wife, somewhat grimly, "This will be the end. You do realise that, don't you?"

The operation at the main city teaching hospital was done quickly, and he was transferred to a less specialised hospital in Birmingham to recover. His care was poor; his deafness made it hard to communicate and there were almost no staff to attend to his needs. Another patient in his bay developed COVID, which meant that Ernie's potential exposure to the virus made it impossible for him to go to a rehab unit. He spent the whole time crying and asking for his wife. He still has nightmares about his time in Heartlands Hospital. He was not allowed to have visitors at any time, and he couldn't hear people calling him on the phone.

With physiotherapy and occupational therapy, he slowly recovered, although some of his care at home had to be privately funded. He said, "I'm not ever going back to that hospital. Please don't make me." Physically, he nearly returned to his pre-fall state, but his short-term memory was faltering. When he unexpectedly passed blood in his stool, he needed the NHS again, and again there was no choice: he had to go back to Heartlands.

After some time in the Medical Assessment Unit, he went to Ward 8, a stroke ward, perhaps not a bad choice for a man with severe mobility problems. He had some blood tests and received a blood transfusion, but none of the tests were necessary to diagnose the cause of the rectal bleeding. They said it was diverticulitis, but of course, they didn't know. He needed a CT scan of the abdomen, which didn't happen.

He had a fall out of bed because he was confused. He hit his head and needed a CT scan, but again, this didn't happen in a timely manner. Nobody from the ward communicated that he had fallen to his wife or his family, and he wasn't medically reviewed for hours because there was one on-call doctor for two stroke wards.

Realising that the NHS sometimes needs a bit of a shove, my wife rang the ward to ask what was being done to make a diagnosis so that he could have specific treatment. The scan was again delayed because nobody made any adjustments to deal with his confusion. Then, ninety-six hours after admission, we were told that both the CT and MRI scanners were broken. My wife asked that Ernie's wife be allowed to visit and was told by the charge nurse that there were no visitors allowed, despite that not being national policy.

She spoke to the ward sister, who also refused to allow a visit. My wife said she wanted to escalate it to the hospital matron. In the meantime, Jenny rang Ernie on the hospital phone, but he was confused, informing her that she needed to take 'the number 5 bus from Calcutta'.

Ernie said to the nurse, "I can't hear, I'm as deaf as a post." He had taken his hearing aid in the ambulance, but the hospital had lost it. A confused elderly person cannot look after their belongings; he is still trying to reclaim the four thousand pounds the hearing aid cost.

Four days after arriving at the hospital, he had no diagnosis, no specific treatment and no continuity of care from his medical team. It was very clear that there was minimal nursing and medical staffing in the ward and that, if he became life-threateningly ill, he was likely to die without his wife seeing him again. To be clear, all the staff we spoke to were polite, helpful and pleasant, doing their best under impossible circumstances. This isn't even the worst of the NHS, but simply typical. We all have experiences like this, but policymakers seem to be unwilling to find the money and resources to fix the problem.

Jenny, my wife, will sometimes have to call twenty times over two hours to get through, and when she does get through, the nurse usually tells her to call back later or the next day. We arrange Zoom calls, but the nurses can't find time to help Ernie with them. Ernie remains confused and sorting him out medically is difficult. He is probably in his last few months of life.

Nobody is allowed to visit, and we fear that his wife will never see him again. My wife rings every day to get progress reports and the doctors are unfailingly polite. There is minimal evidence of consultant input and no sense of urgency. It's just not good enough. Ernie deserves better.

# Chapter 6
# Stories from the NHS

*There is no point in writing about the NHS. Nobody wants to hear you criticise it. You don't have the right.*

*Being part of the NHS is like being a member of the Communist Party: show dissent and it will be noted, and you will be dealt with. As an individual, no matter how good you are, you don't matter, and you can be discarded.*

*The NHS is the UK's pet dog. We are very fond of it, but we constantly treat it poorly. We yell at it, we sometimes even kick it. Despite our habitual abuse, we are surprised when it is broken, and we do little to fix it. We expose it to intolerable pressure, and when it survives, just, we celebrate, without pausing to think about how unpleasant it is for the staff to work for the NHS.*

*"The British National Health Service is socialist medicine, which I don't like. Patients don't have much choice and everybody is paid the same, irrespective of how good they are or how hard they work. The whole system is underfunded and there is no reward for excellence." (An American colleague)*

## The National Health Service: First encounters

I completed my postgraduate medical and research training in Australia in 1990, having spent my first eight years as a doctor there, completing my Fellowship of the Royal Australasian College of Physicians[3] and submitting my PhD thesis. Like many doctors from Australia, I came to the UK to get a broader experience, to work in a world-renowned unit at one of the great London

---

[3] This is the equivalent of MRCP (Membership of the Royal College of Physicians): a requirement to obtain a consultant physician post in a hospital and also enables one to undergo specialist training. It involves rigorous written and clinical examinations. The pass rate is only 40%, many candidates require several attempts before passing

hospitals, to experience London life, and to travel to mainland Europe as often as possible. However, unlike many Australians, I was not set on returning: I had decided jobs would determine where I went next. To achieve my goals, I had to prioritise my career, and at that time there were more opportunities in Europe and the US than in Australia.

The Hammersmith Hospital had an unremarkable appearance and basic facilities: it was grey and ugly, with various shades of concrete with a stolid Victorian entrance. That did not deter me because there has never been any correlation between the appearance of a British hospital and the quality of the medicine practised within. This was especially true in the early 1990s: many of the great British haematologists such as Dacie and Galton had worked there, and it had become famous for the treatment of chronic myeloid leukaemia (CML). A succession of Australians had worked in the haematology unit, often enhancing their careers. Presenting a patient at the hospital Grand Round was a formative experience, in front of twenty eminent professors sitting in the front row of the main lecture theatre.

The Bone Marrow Transplant Coordinator post I wanted wasn't formally advertised or interviewed for, but it was very sought after by doctors from the UK and overseas. My job application in 1990 predated email, so communication was by letters and phone calls from Australia, sometimes in the middle of the night. On a holiday to Europe, I decided to travel to the UK and was given time to meet the professor. I sat opposite the great man in a room barely big enough to hold two torn green vinyl chairs, our knees nearly touching. He was tall, with thinning grey hair and no tie, which was unusual in those days.

I had been warned that he was different. No pleasantries were exchanged and indeed, for the first two minutes, almost no words at all. Time passed slowly while I waited, and he did nothing to make me feel comfortable. That was part of the 'test', I subsequently learnt. The professor eventually made the briefest eye contact and said wearily, "Tell me a bit about yourself."

I prepared thoroughly for interviews but found it hard to work out what he wanted to know. I told him about my training, the places where I had worked, my laboratory research and my scientific papers. He looked a little bored. The interview finished about ten minutes later, and I was told that I would hear the outcome in due course. Subsequently, I found out that Junia, the head of his scientific laboratory, persuaded him to offer me the job, mainly because I had a first-authored paper from my PhD published in the Journal of Clinical

Investigation, a high-impact scientific journal. It had nothing to do with my uncle having worked there twenty years earlier because the professor hadn't liked my uncle.

What do I remember about this august London teaching hospital? At the age of 32, I was appointed to a senior registrar post and ran the transplant unit (Dacie ward) with a registrar and a junior doctor. These junior colleagues weren't run-of-the-mill doctors, as they liked to remind me. My registrar Alan was a delightful Scottish chap, who was very good clinically.

However, all he wanted to do was talk about science and the new discipline of molecular biology, particularly 'homeobox genes'. He also had a weakness for gossip, particularly about liaisons between doctors and nurses. After finishing his clinical training, he moved to a nearly full-time job in the haematology research labs in Cambridge. His very first publication was a first-authored paper in the journal *Cell*, arguably the world's most prestigious science journal—you have to do something totally novel to get a paper in there.

The first junior doctor assigned to the transplant service was an extroverted Northerner from Hull who had a bit of a chip on his shoulder. He liked telling people how he got the job at the Hammersmith. After applying for this highly rated (golden) London rotation, he faced a panel of interviewers, nearly all of whom had been to Oxford or Cambridge (he had looked them up). One of them said, in the snottiest voice imaginable, "I believe you did your initial training in Leeds … how was it?" apparently with a look of distaste on his face.

Raj had prepared for this. He said, "Yes, it was good. In my two years, there I was taught by three Fellows of the Royal Society (FRS). Given that none of you has FRS, I consider that I have had better training in Leeds than I would have had here."

They were shocked and, according to Raj, so impressed by his confidence that they offered him the job. He was even more arrogant than they were, something they rarely encountered.

Every senior haematology registrar was expected to present a patient at the Grand Round. This involved making overhead transparencies of the patient's history, physical findings, tests and treatment with a review of the relevant literature. The Hammersmith Grand Round was famous, even by London teaching hospital standards. A notable case was chosen, the patient was usually present to answer questions, and it was meant to reflect cutting-edge practice. Fortunately, I had a good case.

Ian, a twenty-one-year-old with CML had received a bone marrow transplant and then went into progressive liver failure due to GVHD caused by the transplant. All the drug treatments for GVHD failed, and we did three liver biopsies, showing that his bile ducts were progressively disappearing (vanishing bile duct syndrome; bile ducts are the tubes running from the liver to the gut along which bile flows). He was going to die of liver failure, so I suggested referring him for a liver transplant. He was fortunate to receive one quickly and it was uncomplicated. Three months later, he had normal liver function and was well.

The title of the Grand Round was 'A tale of two transplants'. Six months after his liver transplant, I presented his case, with him sitting beside me on stage. I enjoyed presenting cases, but this was very important, and I was nervous. The eminent professors in the front row of the lecture theatre scowled at me. They wore dark suits and conservative ties. They worked in different departments in the hospital and didn't want to acknowledge that the haematology department had done something well. Ian's life had been saved by doing something that had never been done before (we had written a paper about him and given an oral presentation about him at the European transplant conference).

One of them asked, "OK, he's obviously survived the liver transplant but how well is he really?"

We thought they might ask this. "Ian, can you tell the audience how you feel?" I asked.

Ian shrugged and said, "Well, I'm a plumber, and I am back working full-time. I recently ran a ten-kilometre race. I wasn't happy with the time, but I'll do better on my next one." They still looked sceptical.

"Ian, is there anything you can't do that you would like to do?" I asked.

"No, not really. I feel OK." My boss looked pleased as we left the lecture theatre.

The nurses in the transplant unit at the Hammersmith came from a mixture of backgrounds. Some had travelled from Australia, New Zealand or nearby Europe, but there were also some nurses from posh London families, whom I felt rather looked down on me. In the main, we got on well because I worked hard and I was clinically sound, and they were highly trained transplant nurses. Many of the nurses could drink six pints of beer in an evening when we went out to the pub. I couldn't and didn't really like to drink more than two or three.

Where did they put it all? Still, they were fun to socialise with and in the intense environment of a transplant unit there was very little anti-doctor sentiment. On my very first day as a doctor, I was given some good advice by a senior surgical registrar. He said, "Work hard for the patients. Show you really care about them. Bring the nurses into the decision-making process, and they'll do pretty much anything for you."

One of my fellow registrars, a rather effete, thin Scottish man, certainly found that to be the case. He was on call for haematology and transplant one weekend, and the ward was fairly empty, so he and a nurse (who had arranged to 'overlap' with him on call) found themselves in one of the spare hospital beds (with the curtains drawn), having rather boisterous sex for about two hours on a Saturday night. There was no WhatsApp in those days, but the nurse managed to communicate her feats to a number of nursing colleagues, some of whom were jealous. The same nurse was asked when she arrived for her shift on the Monday afternoon, whether she had heard the news: 'pretty boy' Gordon (not his real name) had just announced that he had got engaged to a girl he met long ago at university. The poor nurse was mortified and had to go home because she couldn't stop crying.

The transplant unit was a tough, stressful environment. Working here also brought me my first encounter with the all-powerful Nurse Manager. In Australia, I was used to running the ward, deciding who would be admitted and who would not. In my early days in London, I decided to admit a patient, only to be countermanded by a senior nurse called Sophie. I was bleeped to her office number (she had her own office).

"Hello, Dr Marks. I'm afraid you can't admit Mr Jones. We've filled the last haematology bed with an elective patient."

"Sophie, the patient I want to admit is really ill with GVHD. He has already waited two days. He has to come in. We can delay the other patient, there'll be a bed tomorrow."

"Dr Marks, the allocation of beds is my decision." She put the phone down.

It was the wrong decision. I think she knew that but did it to demonstrate her power. I went to my boss, the professor, to explain the situation and asked incredulously if she had the power to overrule me. He nodded, saying, "Yes, I am afraid she does." He suggested to me that next time I should try to be more charming! (The patient with GVHD was admitted the next day, after a most uncomfortable night.) After a few months, however, Sophie and I developed a mutual respect for each other.

After six months on the job, I went to the professor to ask if I could have a week off. He had obviously seen this look of desperation before. Before I had entered the room, he said, somewhat in jest, that I could have anything I wanted, except a holiday. If I was not there, the consultants would have to cover me, and they weren't going to do that. It was an intense year at the Hammersmith, transplanting about fifty patients, being responsible for all of their transplant work up and care, and very little respite.

It was exhausting, working from 8:00 am until late in the evening. However, the quality of the medicine was excellent and the experience of working at one of the world's best transplant units turned me into a confident, independent transplanter. After this year, it was clear to me that I should continue in this relatively new field. This has turned out to be a good career decision.

## A final assessment

Due to COVID, the popularity of the NHS has never been higher. In 2020–2021, doctors and nurses worked under great pressure and risked their lives looking after COVID patients, sometimes without adequate protective equipment. It has been reported that over one hundred thousand NHS staff have long-term symptoms of the virus (long COVID) and many more have post-traumatic stress disorder.

As an institution, the NHS is admired for doing a good job under very difficult circumstances. To be clear, I am committed to a universally available, centrally funded health system. The best thing is that the NHS doesn't differentiate between rich and poor people: they get the same care. But what is the NHS like to work in?

When I leave the NHS, the thing I will miss most is the patients. The struggles they go through, their courage, their desire to be cured and how most of the time they manage to be nice. I will miss the nurses I work with their talent, their skill and the way they find time to look after patients' emotional needs. Some of them, and I can't name them (but they know who they are), are simply brilliant: highly trained, knowledgeable and perceptive. I will also miss a lot of my medical colleagues and their steadfastness and desire to do good. I will miss the banter and the black humour that you encounter on a ward round or during a team meeting.

One thing I definitely will not miss, however, is the smell of hospitals. You become immune to it; your olfactory system ignores it. When I return from a two-week holiday, I am again able to sense the quite horrible smell of the wards. It's hard to describe because it varies. Sometimes, it's sweaty patients; sometimes urine, faeces or vomit.

Almost as bad is the smell of the food the patients receive: overcooked vegetables, sometimes burnt food, horrible sauces and gravy. The food the NHS serves patients is poor, partly because we don't spend enough money on it. Our cancer patients constantly complain about the food. Eating is an important part of getting better, but hospital food is so unappetising that they can't eat.

Meetings are also not a strength of the NHS, although the way we use them changed with the pandemic. Few meetings are productive, and they take forever to organise. A productive meeting needs a strong chair and a clear, agreed agenda. All of us attend meaningless meetings that make no decisions, 'gabfests' at which we talk about the problems but don't really propose any solutions because that would mean more resources. The culture of the NHS is that one should not ask for more money but continue to struggle.

People circle around each other, not really addressing the problems but avoiding future trouble by having 'discussed' things, identifying glaring deficiencies and possibly putting an issue on the 'risk register'. If it is on the risk register, you can avoid blame because you can say that there was no money to address the problem or that other risks had a higher priority.

For example, when our transplant ward moved to its current site ten years ago, we did a lot of work to show that we needed at least twenty-five haematology and transplant beds. The hospital decided to 'give' us twenty-two; they thought this would save money. Our unit is constantly full and overflows into other wards. The result of this lack of beds is that our patients have their curative treatment delayed and when patients come in with emergency problems, they are admitted to wards staffed by people that don't have the specialist skills to look after them. At the time, I was the Director of the Bone Marrow Transplant (BMT) unit and was involved in all the planning meetings, which occurred over two years.

The planning group met repeatedly and agreed we needed at least three more beds. The hospital stalled, saying there was no money. One manager said to me privately, "If you keep asking for twenty-five beds you will put the whole project at risk; it may not happen at all." We actually had to move because the adult transplant unit was co-located within the children's unit and some of the parents had complained that it wasn't appropriate for their children to be in the same building as adults. This was heavy-handed management: the experienced managers just wore us down and got their way.

"If you show that over a period of time that you need the extra beds, you will get them," we were told, but that simply wasn't true. We needed the beds from the day we moved in, and we didn't get them. About ten years later we got two additional beds, but only because we started doing CAR-T-cell therapy.

We filled in incident forms when patient care was compromised, and eventually, the lack of haematology and transplant beds was put on the trust 'risk register'. Filling in the incident forms was meaningless and time-consuming because nothing was done about the problem, but it made the managers feel that they had addressed the issue. I can't tell you how annoying it is to work in an organisation that thinks this way. The money should have been found and the problem avoided.

The hospital IT system also deserves a mention. You wouldn't believe how bad and how conservative it is. The computers we use are years out of date and until 2021 used operating systems such as Internet Explorer 8, which was released in 2009. Some days I spend eight hours working on my computer, so it really matters. Slow or malfunctioning computers commonly prolong my working day.

One day, I came into work and logged on. Emblazoned across the screen was: 'University Hospitals Bristol named Digital exemplar in the South-West!' This was astonishing. God help the hospitals that were following our example. For years, the IT department's firewall blocked webcasts, and they still will not officially support Zoom, even though half the world uses it.

The computers are ponderously slow. We are told to turn our computers off every night, but if you do that it can take you more than ten minutes to restart in the morning. The junior doctors in our unit who have recently worked overseas say it is much better elsewhere.

By far the worst thing, however, is the attitude that every penny should be saved. I totally disagree. What matters most is delivering excellent patient care and looking after the very stressed staff. This meanness permeates the entire NHS and makes it a very difficult employer to work for. NHS managers probably monitor the number of paperclips we use.

There is suspicion about everything you ask for and sometimes it takes so long to achieve change that you run out of energy. The result of this is often mediocrity, contentment with meeting national targets, not getting into trouble, but also seldom being outstanding. So, the response to almost every proposed change that would cost money is 'no'.

Perhaps the best example of this reluctance to spend money came when I was the administrative director of the transplant unit. I held this post for a number of years and constantly wanted to improve things. We had near-hospital accommodation for the transplant patients and their families, in an old hospital building on three floors. Some of the patients weren't strong enough to walk up the stairs, so I asked the general manager for a stairlift. "Lucy, can we please find the money for the stairlift? Some of the patients are effectively trapped in their rooms. If they go downstairs, they can't go back up."

The general manager replied, "If you write a business case, we'll consider it." Classic stalling: she thought I wouldn't have the time to write the business case.

"Why does it need a business case? This is about enabling disabled patients to have access to the hospital accommodation that their referring hospital is paying for."

She replied, "That's the way we do things in this department. It will also need a risk assessment."

One of the risks was that the patients might fall down the stairs. After endless meetings with managers over nearly two years, a new equipment request going out to three suppliers for quotes and a risk assessment, I gave up and financed the stair-lift from scarce patient-donated funds for about £9,000. This was not what the funds were intended for: they were largely donated by the families of patients who had died under my care. Previously, we had spent this charitable money on making patient accommodation more pleasant: nicer curtains, duvets, sofas, kitchen equipment and so on.

The NHS had a responsibility to make its estate accessible to patients, but it did everything it could to avoid spending money. NHS managers are taught to be very grudging in funding new projects. If you really need it, you will ask again, and again … or you will give up. Doctors aren't managers: it isn't part of our training. We do management in addition to our clinical work and never have much time to spend on it.

Another example involves the time when we were setting up our new CAR-T-cell service, and because these patients get severe neurological complications, we needed neurology support from our neighbouring hospital in Bristol because our hospital doesn't have a neurology department. We had to 'negotiate' the cost of that service and wouldn't be accredited if we didn't have a signed service level agreement (SLA) for them to provide urgent neurology input. Would the neurologists attend four half-day sessions or three-and-a-half? Of course, it simply didn't matter; it was transferring money from one part of the NHS to another. Who could possibly care?

I asked my general manager, "Sophie, does it really matter if we pay North Bristol five thousand pounds a year more? We won't be able to do CAR T-cells until we have a contract."

She said, "David, this needs to be negotiated, and you will have to be patient until we agree on a cost."

Various staff members bickered and haggled, threatening each other to not provide the service and repeatedly refusing to sign the service level agreement (SLA) over several months. What a waste of everybody's time. The managers felt they had to fight over every penny: that was their culture. (Subsequently, the service they provided was much less than four sessions, but they used this money to fund another consultant. It was a real struggle to get them to come to our hospital.) The NHS can be so exhausting to navigate.

## Achieving change

My efforts to change things in my hospital constitute one of the great frustrations of my professional career. In my thirty years of working in the NHS, I have found that it is not good at change. At times, change is actively resisted, despite being one of my hospital trust's 'core values'. Indeed, one of the core values of the NHS constitution is to 'actively seek better ways of working to achieve improvements', and obviously all hospitals need to constantly change in order to respond to an ever-changing medical environment.

I think I have achieved fewer than ten major changes in my twenty-seven-year career as a senior consultant. Of course, these changes were achieved by many other people. Starting CAR-T-cell therapy at the hospital is an example. This didn't really emanate from us; we were approached by NHS England to apply to be one of the six CAR-T-cell centres. The hospital simply had to do this and, when it decided to commit to changing, was quite good at it.

My colleague Rachel, who is a far better manager than I am, led this process, and we are now a big CAR-T-cell centre. Another change was starting cord blood transplants, way back in 2001. My paediatric colleagues were doing these transplants so I just decided to start a program (you couldn't do this nowadays, there would be endless discussions and it would take years to happen).

Change requires energy, thought and planning. It's not comfortable. Initially, it's easiest to not make changes. Changes commonly involve expenditure, seen by many as evil. In the NHS, you are up against innate conservatism.

## The UK National Health Service: Mixed feelings

Everybody in the UK has an opinion about the NHS and all but the very elderly have grown up with it. I have worked in it for thirty years. I don't have the same (almost biological) feelings about it: I am able to look at it more objectively and see its weaknesses, and I don't have the same emotional attachment to it. The NHS is good in many ways, but it could be so much better.

It's like a wounded animal that we keep resuscitating. We mercilessly batter it, even though many of us love it. Almost as a policy, we under-resource it, but then we expect it to cope somehow. The COVID pandemic is a good but extreme example. In 2020, when we realised that about a quarter of all patients admitted to hospitals with the virus would require the intensive care unit, we found out that Germany had five times as many ITU beds per capita as the UK.

Five times as many: one of us has got it wrong. Not to worry, though: 'the NHS will cope'. Of course, it didn't, so we needed to build temporary (Nightingale) hospitals and import and manufacture ventilators, in huge quantities, in record time. There was probably higher mortality than there should have been, and in many hospitals, there were days of near-panic. Some hospitals were on the verge of running out of oxygen.

The grossly underfunded national intensive care network is the result of deliberate government policy. Not having a reserve capacity is cheap and, for most of the time, just enough, but every winter there are too few beds to deal with 'winter pressures'. Put another way, the health system is in a constant state of crisis. Why would anybody want to run things this way? It's dangerous to patients and stressful for staff.

And yet, you can't help blaming yourself when the system doesn't measure up. Criticising the NHS itself is not tolerated. You can suggest improvements, but you can't say things are suboptimal. If I criticised my hospital publicly, I would be disciplined. The staff do their absolute best for patients no matter where they come from, and it's free at the point of care. That's why British people love it: they get a reasonable health service without seeming to pay for it (although, of course, we do pay for it through taxes and national insurance).

These flaws also create conflict between doctors and nurses, and managers. NHS doctors want to do the best for patients, but we can't. Meanwhile, many managers see it as their job to actively stop us from spending money and using resources. Health systems require constant revision and the money shortage makes necessary change hard to implement. All private organisations have to change; remaining static isn't an option.

This means that what we deliver isn't always world-class. It's not a popular observation, but survival rates of the major cancers (colon, breast and lung), for example, are significantly worse than many of our neighbouring countries that spend more on health (e.g. https://www.cancerresearchuk.org/health-professional/cancer-statistics/statistics-by-cancer-type/bowel-cancer/survival#heading-Five). For most people this doesn't matter, but when 'you' get colon cancer, it really does.

You have a lower chance of being cured here in the UK, but that's not because the doctors are better in Germany or France, but rather that other countries have better health systems (again, Germany, France and Australia come to mind) with stronger policies, planning and care delivery. Through various means, they have more money in their system (in part from private funding) and this translates into more resources, more rapid diagnoses and better outcomes.

## Inadequate resources: A urological experience in the NHS

I could have included this in the chapter 'Being a patient' but the story has much more to do with the NHS than with me. As a patient, I have had too many encounters with urologists. My problems have been managed in three hospitals. I have two separate urological problems: recurrent kidney stones and benign enlargement of the prostate, which made at times has made it difficult for me to pass urine. Nearly all men over sixty have some degree of prostatism.

In spring 2019, I had a road bike accident in Majorca and had to cut short the holiday and return to the UK to have surgery on a broken thumb with a ruptured tendon. (I cycled into a roadside drain, which I couldn't see, and went over the handlebars.) I also had broken ribs and had lots of facial abrasions. I became dehydrated after the accident, which caused a urinary tract infection, and required strong painkillers, which made my bladder outlet unable to relax.

When I returned early to Bristol, I was in severe pain, with urinary retention causing a distended bladder and was having rigors due to a high temperature. I went to the hospital where I work for treatment. It doesn't have a dedicated urology department, but its A&E deals with urological emergencies.

An administrator at reception took my details and, although I looked terrible, it took forty-five minutes for me to be assessed by an emergency triage nurse. She said I needed a cubicle in the 'majors' section of the A&E department but told me that there were 'no beds and no staff'. I was led into a dank, poorly lit corridor at the back of A&E where I was tenth in line, sitting on a chair, with my wife (and all the other carers) sitting on the floor.

We were told that it was not possible to say when I would be seen. Nobody checked how I was, took observations (blood pressure, pulse or temperature) or offered me pain relief. The other people in the corridor received no attention either, and there was no sign of movement in the queue.

My shaking was getting worse, and I was feeling faint, so we rang a medical friend who works at the other major hospital in Bristol to see if he could help and got my son to drive us there. We told him the story, and he said, "Yeah, you had better come here; we couldn't be any worse. Let me know if you don't get seen reasonably soon."

This other hospital's A&E department was much less busy, but I still had to wait another seventy-five minutes just to get some pain relief.

None of the other people in the waiting area at Southmead was treated any better than me. A lot of them looked really ill and it is likely that some of them also needed urgent care. There was a mixture of young and old patients. Some had obvious injuries with arms in slings, ankles swathed in bandages or in moon boots; there were people holding their tummies and groaning, while others were pale and listless.

They sat impatiently on narrow plastic seats, in obvious discomfort. Some of the younger people, after a while, lay on the floor. However, it is hard to care about other people when you are ill.

About five hours after first arriving at the hospital, I was catheterised for urinary retention. I then waited more than three hours in A&E before being admitted to a hospital bed upstairs. I was given nothing to eat, and it wasn't even possible to go to the toilet; they were so understaffed. I was in bad pain and had low blood pressure due to a severe infection.

None of my treatment was timely. People with infections severe enough to cause low blood pressure like I had should receive antibiotics within an hour, as they are likely to have bacteria in their blood, which can be life-threatening; low blood pressure was probably the cause of my faintness. After four hours, I was given antibiotics, but it took me days to recover from this ordeal.

I was in the hospital for two days; it was impossible to go home when the discharge decision was made because there was no discharge summary and no discharge medication. The junior doctor who was responsible for this had never met me and was paged repeatedly for four hours. I virtually wrote the summary for her on my laptop, but even with all the delays, the drugs I needed were not ready. I was sent home without antibiotics or pain relief, the two main reasons I was admitted.

My wife came back the next day to pick up the discharge medication, and they still weren't ready. She waited two-and-a-half further hours at the pharmacy. The only positive aspect of my experience was a conversation with my locum consultant, who was very kind and knowledgeable; he came to my room and spent some time with me explaining things. He really cared although, of course, he may have given me more time with me because I was a consultant colleague.

Overall, it was a really poor hospital experience in terms of efficiency and medical processing. Some of the medical care was fine, but some was pretty ignorant and unsafe. It's bad enough being ill without all the delays. I had bacteria in my blood; not being treated promptly was dangerous. I considered making a formal complaint, but I didn't think it would do any good; they would just blame it on a lack of resources.

I would hope that we have never treated any of my patients as badly as this. A number of my medical and non-medical friends have read this: none are surprised and most describe it as a 'typical' NHS experience. I have had time to reflect further on this episode and conclude that if there was any lasting harm, I would have been very angry and might have considered legal action. The hospitals could not have defended their care: it was substandard. However, the reason I have told this story is to show how inadequate the NHS can be, and that we should all be asking our government to provide the funding to improve it. We will all need the NHS one day. If we accept this under-resourcing, this is the standard of care we can expect.

## A&E again

My second bike accident in two years. I went over a speed bump slowly, landed leaning to the right and then fell on my right side, causing abrasions, probably breaking a rib and damaging my back. The back pain has got worse: that's why I am at A&E again, to get an X-ray and some advice. It's 9:00 am on Sunday, and ten people are crowded into a narrow, elongated room with about forty plastic seats, half of them blocked off by red and white tape to enforce social distancing. When I book in, the apologetic senior nurse (who has seen it all) tells me that the patients waiting have been there for up to seven hours, some from last night.

"Can I ask if any of the patients have symptoms of COVID? If they do, my immune system isn't normal, and I don't really want to sit with them," I said.

"No, I don't think so. Why don't you sit at the end of the room, away from them?"

Even if they did have viral symptoms there wouldn't be enough space to separate everybody. I find a plastic seat in front of the toilets and look around me. Dishevelled people are lying across three very uncomfortable seats, wearing last night's clothes, stained by blood, alcohol or vomit. They are bleary-eyed but not at all cross, because this is what they expect from the NHS. Some of them periodically go up to reception and ask how long it will be until they are seen, and the nurse says she doesn't know.

They will get good care when they are seen, but there will be lots of waiting in the queue, in very uncomfortable circumstances. The waiting area is grubby, small and unwelcoming. I think that might be deliberate. After being triaged, I am put in a cubicle at the back of A&E because of a past antibiotic-resistant urinary infection. This is not necessary, and I may be receiving preferential treatment. I don't feel too guilty, mainly because I am in pain, and perhaps it's OK for doctors to be seen rapidly if it doesn't compromise other people's treatment.

"Professor Marks, can you come with me? I believe you had a bike accident. Can you tell me what happened?"

The A&E fellow who sees me is polite and focused, examines me carefully, and explains his reasoning well. He is a good doctor. There's never been an issue with doctor quality at the good hospitals in the UK. The problem is the number of doctors and nurses, and the pressure we are all under.

A&E has not changed since these recent encounters; in fact, the waits are even longer.

# Chapter 7
# Stories of Sadness

## Miles

Miles was charming, a tall, thin man in his early twenties diagnosed with ALL just before Christmas 2015. He had light brown hair, a posh accent and was vegan, something not always catered for by the NHS. He became ill during his second year of studying linguistics at Manchester University. When he was told that the treatment involved three years of intensive therapy and lots of hospital visits, he decided to return to Bristol so he could live at home and be looked after by his family, deferring his university course.

Miles was quite rebellious and idealistic. He had been a boarder at Eton and was expected to go to Oxford but decided that those goals were not worthwhile. When he first arrived at the hospital, he was with a girlfriend from his school days, who had recently started a demanding course at Oxford. She was a delightful, quiet, very bright girl and it was easy to see the chemistry between them. They decided to split up while I knew Miles but remained close friends.

I first met Miles in the teenage and young adult unit in our cancer centre, with his mother and girlfriend. I introduced myself, and he said, "Is it OK if I call you David?"

I'm never one for formality in my professional relationships with patients; it just gets in the way. Some are not happy with calling me by my first name: most of them call me 'Prof'. Miles was establishing some ground rules, showing that he wanted to share the decision-making. He agreed to be treated on the UK national trial for young patients with ALL and achieved an excellent remission after his first course of chemotherapy.

This consisted of four drugs and about two weeks as an inpatient in the hospital. During the second course, he developed severe abdominal pain, which was found to be due to a rare bowel problem (intussusception), which resulted in him needing to have half his colon removed. It wasn't due to his leukaemia. I arrived on the ward on a Monday and my registrar told me what happened in my absence.

"Fucking hell, we were doing so well. This could be really significant." I was so upset: there are so many ways of snatching defeat from the jaws of victory. Miles's chemotherapy was interrupted for three weeks while he recovered from the abdominal surgery, and I have always wondered if this might be the reason the leukaemia relapsed, although my paediatric colleagues assured me that studies had shown that this didn't matter.

Miles's leukaemia took two years to come back and was very hard to detect because it didn't relapse in his bone marrow. It was only in his bones: we found this on a special positron emission tomography (PET) scan. I got him back into remission with a new antibody called inotuzumab, and he went on to have a bone marrow transplant. Only hundred days after the transplant, he accompanied me on the train to Manchester to attend a meeting that decided whether the drug he had received on a compassionate basis (inotuzumab) would be funded by the NHS for other patients with ALL.

He was a powerful patient advocate and spoke eloquently. I knew he would be persuasive, and he was. He wanted to help other people, not just focus on himself. I was uncertain about letting him come to Manchester on a train (he wore a mask), as it was a significant sacrifice for somebody recovering from a transplant.

The leukaemia came back again about six months after the transplant in his cerebrospinal fluid, causing nerve palsies that made his face lopsided. I tried to send him to Philadelphia for CAR-T-cell treatment (privately funded) but this was not straightforward. The unit in America that had cured a previous patient of mine took a long time to process things, and at that time, CAR T-cells were not available in the UK. I treated Miles with chemotherapy into his spinal fluid, some more inotuzumab and radiotherapy to the brain, but the leukaemia kept coming back and Miles eventually made the decision to have no further therapy. This was entirely reasonable and didn't require detailed discussion.

In the three years, I looked after Miles, we had several conversations that had nothing to do with his leukaemia. He was very involved in green issues and was a committed, ideological vegan. He liked ideas and would ring up friends to talk late into the night, even quite close to his death. Near the end when he had stopped treatment, I checked to see that he was comfortable and to ask if he had any questions. I was going to be away for part of the following week, and we both knew we would probably not see each other again. We didn't say goodbye.

Unusually, I went to his funeral and met and talked to lots of his friends, realising how much he would be missed. The wake was in the gardens of his family's country house in Wiltshire, with views of the countryside for miles in every direction. It was a beautiful, hazy sunny day. We all did Miles's favourite walk along a narrow grassy path through a copse of plane trees. Everybody spoke of how special he was and how he had changed them.

Miles was expected to get a job that made lots of money and had a difficult relationship with his father, who looked at life very differently. Miles hoped to invent something and start his own business, and I'm sure he would have done so. Very sadly, his father died in a riding accident a few months before Miles died, leaving his mother with an intolerable burden of grief. Some close friends of ours know her well, and we remain in touch.

## Postscript: Letter to Miles's mother after his death

*Dear Henrietta,*

*We are returning from France today. Maria texted me to let me know that Miles had died. I am very sorry to hear this. We, you and Miles all tried very hard, but it was not to be. You will probably have many questions remaining and part of the reason for writing is to say that if you would like to come and see me in the next few weeks, that's fine; I am sure we can find a time. Many families do this, but I will leave it up to you.*

*When one of my leukaemia patients dies, I always look back and ask if we could have done things better. In Miles's case, except for a few minor things, I think the answer is 'no'. From the point of his relapse, we were never in complete control. Only 20% of adults who have relapsed ALL survive. The problems we had resulted from a lack of the tools that would have enabled us to recognise that Miles's ALL, which we classified as low-risk, was in fact high-risk. The national ALL group I belong to is currently doing some whole genome sequencing studies that should enable us to recognise this better.*

*Finally, I wanted to share with you my impressions of Miles. He was such a remarkable, thoughtful and clever young man. I had many conversations with him, some of them nothing to do with his illness; he was great fun to talk to. He was kind and unusually aware of the feelings of the people around him. I shall not forget him.*

*This won't help Miles, but I have learnt lots of things from looking after him, and we will get better at treating ALL patients like him. I'm sure we will talk again soon.*

*David*

## A surprise in outpatients

Ian was one of my most grateful patients. He had high-risk AML that was not in a deep remission after chemotherapy, and which therefore needed a transplant. Because his tissue type was rare, he didn't have a sibling or unrelated donor, so his best stem cell options were cells from two cord blood units. However, that's a transplant we normally do in younger patients, and Ian was fifty-nine. It was a risky transplant, with perhaps a 30% chance of him not surviving.

Ian was chubby, ruddy-faced and not particularly fit. He wasn't well during the transplant inpatient stay, with moderate GVHD, but he survived and on day 100 was in remission and recovering. I allowed him to go home and agreed to share his care with his local haematologist, seeing him every three months in Bristol. He had very few problems over the next two years.

At two-and-a-half years out, Ian turned up to the clinic with his wife, looking pretty well. My previous note from the two-year visit noted he was cycling up to twenty-eight miles per ride (a lot of my patients know how keen I am on cycling; we share stories and some have given me bits of cycling kit as presents).

"Ian, Sarah, how are things going? Are you well?" Unusually Sarah answered, quite briefly.

"We're fine."

I usually start off with a social enquiry, something informal. "Been out on the bike much?"

"No, hardly been out, the weather has been terrible. What about you?"

"I've been out a lot, I'm training for London to Paris, not quite fit enough yet, but it's going OK."

In fact, the weather had been fine (for England) but I didn't take much notice of this. Ian reported slight discomfort in his left loin, but no other symptoms. His weight was stable. I didn't examine him (I probably should have) and we concluded the consultation on a mainly social level. I arranged to see him in four months. If you are well and in remission more than two-and-a-half years after a transplant for acute leukaemia, you are usually cured.

Two hours later, I got a call from the lab registrar, saying Ian's platelet count had dropped to 30 (normal is 150) and his blood film was full of leukaemic blasts. Quite out of the blue, his leukaemia had relapsed. Ian was on his way home, on the M5 and driving, so I called his referring haematologist so he could arrange to see Ian the following day, to break the news and make plans.

"Hi, Simon, this is David. I've just seen Ian. He looked OK, but I'm afraid I have some bad news. His platelets have fallen, and our lab registrar has seen lots of blasts on the blood film. He was well but hasn't been out cycling, which is a bit unusual, and he had some left loin pain. Not sure why."

"We'll bring him in for a marrow to confirm it. Is it worth trying to get him back into remission?"

"Well, given it is a late relapse he has a chance of going into remission and if he does, a second transplant has about a 25% chance of working. The first transplant was tough (and he only had cord blood donors), so he may not want to do this, I'd leave it up to him. Sorry, such a nice guy," I finished, somewhat irrelevantly.

The referring consultant and I discussed giving Ian strong re-induction chemotherapy, but we both knew that achieving a good remission was unlikely and that he would probably die in the next few weeks. I went home, feeling sad and desolate. These things happen: treatments fail and people die, but this was a man I thought we had cured. I felt guilty that I was unable to tell him myself that the leukaemia has come back: it was my responsibility because the treatment we had delivered had failed to cure him.

## We're not having sex

It was two years after the transplant, and I was doing a thorough check of how Mia was doing. She had had a bit of GVHD, so I was checking there weren't any unforeseen, extra complications; I always warn my patients that GVHD can affect nearly any part of the body. She was back at work part-time work and her kids were attending school after a long absence during the pandemic. (They stayed at home to reduce the chance of acquiring COVID and passing it on to Mia.) Her husband was working full-time, and I never saw him at virtual appointments. Mia seemed to be well; she had taken charge of her illness and was letting her family get on with life.

"Mia, where is the skin sore or inflamed?"

"A few places, my tummy and my legs."

"Anywhere else?"

"Well, it does affect me down below."

"Do you mean your vulva and your vagina?"

"Yes."

"Is it sore inside the vagina?" She nodded. She was not embarrassed and was gently smiling. She trusted me and had always called me David. "I'm going to need to ask you some personal questions."

She nodded.

"Is it painful when you have sex?"

She answered slowly, "We're not having sex."

"Not at all?" She nodded again. "When was the last time?"

"Before the transplant."

I couldn't help myself. "Oh, my goodness. Not for two years? I feel very remiss not having asked you about this before."

"It's OK, David, I'm alive and my family is fine."

"Is it just the discomfort?" She shook her head.

"No, I just don't feel like it. It doesn't really matter."

"Well, I think it does. You're forty-two and way too young to be hanging up your boots, in my opinion. I'd like to look into it if that's OK."

She nodded.

"What does your husband think?"

"He's very understanding."

That made me feel so guilty that I had missed something so basic. I had even less excuse because I had done two studies of sexual dysfunction in transplant patients when I was working in Philadelphia, both published in the journal *Bone Marrow Transplantation*. There was a very good psychology department at the US hospital and the professor of psychology had devised his own, widely used questionnaire that quantified and described sexual dysfunction. We did a retrospective study that showed that nearly half of all transplant patients had sexual issues and that these problems were largely unrecognised. Most doctors don't ask transplant patients about sexual issues, and patients don't tend to volunteer these symptoms.

We are too focused on keeping the patient alive, avoiding relapse and treating GVHD. In fact, sexual problems often arise from GVHD, either through direct effects on pelvic organs, changes in body image or side effects of medication. It's often due to more than one problem and sometimes there is a loss of sexual desire due to tiredness, depression and a change of life priorities.

It matters. It's not normal to go from having regular sex to none at all; it changes relationships and is one of the reasons why some marriages end during or after transplant therapy. Sexual problems require specialist diagnosis and intervention, and it isn't easy to find the right person to which to refer a patient. A gynaecologist saw Mia and thought that GVHD might be part of the cause, but then realised there was a loss of libido.

This latter issue would require some exploration, and possibly some sessions with her husband. The outcome of these interventions is uncertain, as there is no systematic study of treating post-transplant sexual dysfunction. We need more research and a roadmap to follow.

In my final virtual consultation with Mia, she was smiling but sad because we both knew it would be goodbye. I said because there was little to lose, "I shouldn't say this, but you are one of my favourite patients." I was concerned that her sexual issues would get lost during the transfer of care.

"You are definitely my favourite doctor," she said.

"Mia, stay well," I said and signed off.


## Sam

Sam was sixteen and had only just finished his GCSE exams when he became ill. His leukaemia team in Wales loved him from the outset, which made it hard for them when things weren't going well. Sam's main interest was rugby and football, and it was all he wanted to talk about. He was six foot two inches and had more than 80 kg of muscle. His older brother was even bigger and an outstanding rugby player, hoping to play for Wales.

Sam was diagnosed with leukaemia (ALL) and was given standard treatment for an adolescent. He responded reasonably well but had small amounts of leukaemia (MRD) present after the first chemotherapy cycle. That's when things went badly wrong. He started the second phase of treatment and became confused after receiving a drug called methotrexate, which was injected into his spinal fluid to prevent leukaemic relapse. This brain malfunction (encephalopathy) made it necessary to delay his treatment, and during those few days, his leukaemia returned with a vengeance.

He restarted treatment, but over a single weekend, his white cell count rose from nine to 57. (The normal white cell count is less than ten.) He was obviously in big trouble. Chemotherapy wasn't working, and we needed to get him into remission to do a transplant, so the only potential way out of this was CAR T-cells. This would only be possible if his leukaemia could be controlled for six weeks. Before the era of CAR T-cells, he would have died very rapidly.

Sam had an outstanding haematology consultant who asked for our input early, so I got involved and, with a lot of chemotherapy and some newer ALL agents, we kept him going until the CAR-T-cell infusion. It was a nerve-racking time, with constant ups and downs. The chemotherapy affected his T-cell count, making it hard to collect sufficient T-cells for transformation into CAR T-cells. Sam also had two wonderful parents: his mother a nurse who was knowledgeable but never interfering and his father a huge caring bear of a man, always asking questions and working with us to get the best outcome. One of them was always by the bedside, watching everything, making sure everything that should happen, did happen.

His outcome was uncertain, so we did 'parallel planning'. Although we were working flat-out to cure him, we also were making plans if things didn't work out. 'Hope for the best but plan for the worst': we now offer this approach to all CAR-T patients. Our specialist transplant and CAR-T-cell CNS saw him with a palliative care nurse and talked to him about dying. He was very clear that he wanted to go ahead with the treatment, to 'die trying' if necessary.

Sam was most worried about how his death would affect his parents and his brother. It was very sad to hear a sixteen-year-old talk about his concern for his family. He also had worked out that he would need to defer his A-levels, knowing that he might never take them.

Because he didn't respond well to chemotherapy, we knew Sam would have high levels of leukaemia at the time of the infusion of the CAR T-cells, so I told him and his parents that he was likely to get quite ill afterwards and need to go to the intensive care unit, probably for a few days. This prediction was correct: he got cytokine release syndrome (CRS) the day after the infusion, with fevers up to nearly 41°. His blood pressure dropped, and he needed careful monitoring. His CRS was treated with tocilizumab, anakinra and steroids. He became confused again, but this rapidly got better.

Sam then developed a rare problem called 'macrophage activation syndrome', which meant he needed red cells, platelets and clotting factors. I contacted some colleagues nationally and in the USA, but there was little experience with this problem. He eventually responded to anakinra and steroids, but unfortunately, it made his inpatient stay a longer, precious time that he had hoped to spend at home with his family.

All of this occurred at the height of the COVID pandemic. Everybody was wearing masks and rigorously practising social distancing. The ICU told us that beds were scarce and that, if he got ill, they might not be able to find a bed for him. Because Sam's leukaemia was so active, we had to go ahead, knowing that he might be exposed to the virus in hospital.

At that time, most patients had no visitors, but because he was a child, one parent was allowed to be in the room with him (never both of them). For all our major conversations, one parent had to tune in by speakerphone. At the most dangerous part of his ITU stay, when there was a major update, I saw both parents in the hospital car park, at a distance.

Before the time of admission, I told him that we would do a marrow biopsy on day 28 and that the results would take several days to come back. We did the marrow biopsy, and the initial assessments showed no leukaemia, but I only wanted to speak to him when we had all the tests back. He wasn't coping with the waiting and uncertainty, and our CNS persuaded me to let her tell him that the first assessments were clear. We did so, but then (predictably) the molecular test showed very low levels of leukaemia.

We had not achieved molecular remission, and he was not going to be cured by the CAR T-cells alone. By this time, the family were back home in Wales and the result was conveyed by videoconference because of the pandemic. Sam sat between his parents, with his brother behind him. Their heads visibly sagged when I told them the result. However, there was still hope: if his leukaemia remained at low levels, we could do a transplant that might cure him.

Sam had some inotuzumab in an attempt to reduce the amount of leukaemia in the bone marrow, but it didn't work. This was not good news, but he went ahead with the transplant in the BMT unit in Wales. This was complicated by a fungal infection, but he was discharged home so he could watch the Welsh rugby team narrowly beat Scotland. His bone marrow test four weeks after the transplant showed he still had leukaemia at low levels. Sam had been given every possible treatment for ALL, but these therapies weren't enough.

He was palliated at home and died about three weeks later. His mum had nursed him and it was unbearably sad for her to watch her son slip away. She sent me a bottle of Welsh whisky to thank me for my care of him. It sits on my mantelpiece as a poignant reminder of the limitations of what we can and can't do.

*This chapter is dedicated to Sam Peard and his parents and brother.*

## Reanna

Why do some patients affect you more than others? Sometimes you just connect with them; they seem to like or respect you. Or somehow you get more involved in their life, the effect the disease has on it and their family. There's nothing wrong with that, but it is important for the physician to recognise these special relationships.

Reanna was one such special person. She was twenty-three, had finished her university course at Bristol and had a good job in HR at a private company. She had lots of close friends from her two schools, Badminton and Bristol Grammar School. Her parents were born in India, but she was more British than Anglo-Indian. I first met her when she was referred for a transplant for Philadelphia-positive ALL. She was thin and very small, full of life and always wore colourful clothes.

We always had good control of her leukaemia—it went straight into remission. But her type of ALL almost always requires a transplant. The problem was the side effects of her leukaemia therapy. While having her initial therapy, she got bad clots on the lung (pulmonary emboli), partly related to her leukaemia and partly due to one of the drugs we use for ALL called asparaginase. This significantly affected her lung function, which previously was normal (she had never smoked). Reanna had no matched siblings, so we did an unrelated donor search and, most unusually, found a fully matched unrelated donor, the first time ever in one of my patients from the subcontinent.

The transplant went well, but she developed GVHD of the skin and gut, which required steroids (white cells from the donor attack the gut lining, making it inflamed). Over time, we were able to reduce the steroids to low doses (around 8 mg of prednisolone, roughly the amount the body makes every day). She was nine months out from transplant and as she was less immune-suppressed, I agreed that she could liberalise her social contacts (she had asked me repeatedly for three months). She was keen to see her friends and go out. It had been so long since she had met people outside her household.

Reanna got RSV, which is very common in the autumn, and very infectious. We don't know how she acquired the virus. She was seen in the Haematology Day Unit and X-rayed. The chest X-ray was very slightly abnormal. The viral swab took two days to come back, and she hadn't started on treatment.

This delay may have mattered, although in fact the antiviral treatment hasn't been shown to work. I was away for the weekend when she was admitted and didn't find out about her situation until Monday. I would have gone in to see her. Her condition changed rapidly as the pneumonia progressed. When she was referred urgently to the ICU, she was decompensating, requiring increasing amounts of oxygen.

She was intubated and her scan showed that about 40–50% of the lungs were involved with pneumonia. We gave her IV ribavirin and immunoglobulin, two of the possible treatments for this virus. There was some effect, a slight reduction in the amount of oxygen she required, and the scan showed some clearing, but there was little chance of recovery because so much of her lungs were affected.

We referred her for ECMO to buy us time (some younger patients with COVID and severe pneumonia have been saved this way).[4] However, Reanna wasn't accepted for this treatment, mainly due to some unpublished evidence suggesting that bone marrow transplant patients have a lower chance of survival. Twenty per cent of children do survive, and she was only just older than this age group. An ECMO consultant travelled from London to see her but didn't call me after the assessment to discuss his decision not to accept her. I still wonder why not.

In terms of managing very ill transplant patients, I am probably the most experienced transplanter in the country. I had no personal experience with ECMO, of course, but I do know what is worth trying. There were many conversations with her parents and her best friend, who was a medical student. They wanted all reasonable measures to be taken but realised she was unlikely to survive. The pneumonia progressed, and we couldn't keep her oxygenated, even with 100% oxygen. We agreed to move to palliation, and she died shortly afterwards.

---

[4] ECMO is extracorporeal mechanical oxygenation, a highly technical and expensive way of oxygenating blood outside the body while the patient's lungs are recovering.

We had a morbidity and mortality review about Reanna. The ITU also did a mortality review, but it didn't really help. The ITU care was exemplary, as was the pastoral care to the family, but there was no real discussion about whether she should have received ECMO or the lack of an evidence base upon which to make a decision. The consultant who chaired the meeting took the view that an expert had come from London, decided against it and that was that. I met with her parents a bit later (at their request, away from the hospital) and we ran through some of these matters.

I told them the slight delay in diagnosis probably did not matter. Understandably, they asked me about liberalising her social contacts, and whether in retrospect I would change my mind (an entirely reasonable question). I explained that we could have isolated her until the end of winter, an additional six months; this seemed unreasonable at the time (of course, now, in the pandemic, many BMT patients have been shielded for over eighteen months) and the rampaging virus that took her from well to moribund in three days was highly unusual.

The family contacted me to speak at a charity ball organised at her old school, about a year after her death. Of course, I couldn't refuse and there were over three hundred people there, many of them Anglo-Indian, and there was home-cooked Indian food, which I love. They raised a lot of money and were desperate for something good to come out of her death. At their request, I talked about the advances in ALL treatment, the new targeted therapies and a new trial we were doing to treat people with RSV.

As we have learnt from the COVID pandemic, viral pneumonia remains a largely unsolved problem but there is real hope that outcomes will improve, although that progress is never quick enough. I said that we learnt from patients such as Reanna and that it made us want to get better. All of that was true, but made me feel tremendously sad for her parents and their terrible loss. Reanna is another patient that I will never forget. It did feel like a failure.

## Welcome to Bristol

We returned in June 1996 from three years of working in America. I arrived at the Bristol Children's Hospital to take up my consultant post in 1996, a few days before Christmas. It was a locum position; the senior clinicians wanted to see how I measured up before appointing me permanently. To be eligible for the substantive appointment, I had to have my Australian training recognised by the Royal College of Pathologists.

This required a huge amount of work and lots of documentation related to every job I had done in Australia. I was in the locum for eighteen months and had to be both productive and unobtrusive. When my appointment became substantive, I worried less about making changes that weren't popular with everybody. You can't make a cake without breaking some eggs.

It was my job to develop and expand the adult transplant unit. I inherited only one transplant inpatient and had to do a ward round on him every day. He was Anglo-Caribbean and thus had a poorly matched unrelated donor. His transplant had failed to take (rejection), and he was terribly ill, with permanently low blood counts and established bacterial and fungal infections.

There was little hope, but I looked after him carefully. Inevitably, he died, with his family at hand. Things could only improve from that point, or so I thought.

I was on call on my second and third nights on the job, but not Christmas Day itself. It was a combined adult and paediatric transplant unit, so I was covering children at night. Nowadays that simply wouldn't happen: only specifically paediatrically trained doctors look after children. They reassured me that there were people to call, and an experienced paediatric registrar was always rostered on with me. However, one night on call, early in the new year, the ward called me at 3:00 am because a six-month-old baby named Jolene had had a cardiac arrest.

The junior doctor said, "Come now, please. She's in Room 1." I had been deeply asleep, but that woke me up.

I grabbed the first clothes I could find and drove to the hospital, parking illegally near the entrance to the Children's Hospital. Ten minutes later, I arrived to find a desperate cardiac resuscitation in progress. Nothing was working: there were no pulses, no output from the heart, and we couldn't reverse the ventricular fibrillation, a serious heart rhythm disturbance. Jolene received a transplant for acute leukaemia only two days ago and had a low platelet count. The only potentially reversible thing I could think of was that the low platelet count might have caused bleeding into the pericardium (cardiac tamponade), compressing it and stopping the heart from contracting properly.

I attempted to aspirate the pericardium with a needle, but no blood was forthcoming. I didn't regret trying and wasn't upset when the post-mortem report mentioned 'minor trauma' to the myocardium caused by my aspiration needle. What was far more traumatic was talking to her parents when we stopped, after forty-five minutes of attempted resuscitation. They were sitting on the sofa, holding each other, crying. I had not met them before, and they were beside themselves. I am pretty experienced at breaking bad news, but this was so unexpected.

"Mr and Mrs Taylor, I'm Dr Marks, one of the transplant consultants. I'm afraid I have some very bad news." Her mother screamed, and I couldn't continue. Her husband said, "What on earth happened?"

"I don't know for sure, but somehow the chemotherapy has affected her heart and it has stopped beating."

I emphasised that we had tried everything and that there would need to be a post-mortem to establish the exact cause of death. We left them to hold their child and grieve. It was now six in the morning. The grey sky over the hospital was lightening and it was very still.

I drove home on empty roads, to shower and make strong coffee. Then I came back to the hospital to tell my colleagues at the morning handover what had happened, rather than waking them to convey the news. There was nothing anybody could do now.

# Chapter 8
# Stories of Hope

## Lizzie

When Lizzie was referred to me for a transplant and advice about her leukaemia, I thought I had almost no hope of curing her. However, we were certainly going to try. She was twenty-seven and had been diagnosed with breast cancer three years previously. She was around five foot six, thin with a big toothy smile. She was a schoolteacher's assistant with a six-year-old child and a devoted, loving husband. Her breast cancer was aggressive and required surgery, radiotherapy and chemotherapy, which had increased her chance of developing another cancer by damaging her DNA and causing secondary acute leukaemia (ALL), with changes in her chromosomes that were associated with a poor prognosis.

She looked up at me from the patient's chair next to the desk. Her husband's chair was close to hers, and he held her hand.

"Liz, this is going to be a marathon. It may take up to a year for you to be well, and you may get GVHD."

She nodded: there was no way she was going to give up. She wanted to be around to look after her child. I advised her referring centre about her chemotherapy, and she got into a deep remission, with no leukaemia detectable. However, she needed a transplant to be cured, so we did a donor search. That was her next bit of bad luck because her siblings didn't match and she had no unrelated donors worldwide.

The best option for her was using two cord units. This was a higher-risk transplant, but cord units may exert a strong anti-leukaemic effect, just right for her high-risk leukaemia. She needed total body radiotherapy, which would mean she had a chance of another breast cancer. There was also a substantial chance of long-term GVHD.

Nothing was straightforward. She had to stay in Bristol for three months and needed immune suppressive drugs for GVHD of the skin and lungs. This made her short of breath, but it eventually responded to treatment, and she was able to resume aerobics and walk her child to school. With her lungs vulnerable and her immune system weak, she wasn't able to return to teaching work because the schoolkids were a constant source of infection. Each winter was a risk for her. Her child continued to go to school and occasionally brought infections home.

About a year ago, she sent a lovely handmade thank you card celebrating the fifth anniversary of the transplant and thanking us for keeping her with her family. She said she was sad that I was retiring. I will miss her, her determination and her refusal to give in. You wouldn't know she had been ill. Some of her skin remains thickened and tethered, but she can exercise.

Her lung function is about 50% of normal, but she is able to do everything she wants to, and all the housework except carrying the vacuum cleaner upstairs. She will require lifelong medical care, and although she remains at risk of other cancers, I am confident her leukaemia is cured. On the day of writing, Lizzie has just tested positive for COVID, but is currently well and may not need antivirals.

## Not fit for transplant

Towards the end of my career, a colleague stopped seeing new transplant patients, and I was asked to cover transplants for patients with myelofibrosis. Myelofibrosis is a rare condition where the marrow becomes replaced with scar tissue and this results in marrow failure or transformation to leukaemia. I was determined that I would only do this for patients with a decent chance of cure. This meant seeing people face-to-face, and the patient I have in mind had no computer at home for virtual consultations.

Patrick lived in the Mendips and drove to Bristol, hoping to leave his car in the Park and Ride then get a bus into the hospital. They didn't accept cash, and he couldn't pay by card because he had no bank account and no credit or debit card. This was very unusual. He got a friend to drive him in.

The referral letter contained no information about his social situation, and I found, when I took his history, that he was only sixty years old (he looked well over seventy). He wore a thick, checked shirt, a woolly hat and stained woollen trousers.

"Patrick, I'm Professor Marks. Can I ask you a few things? What do you do for a living?"

"I'm not well enough to work at the moment, but I train horses."

"Who lives with you at home?"

"I live alone in my caravan, which is in a friend's field. I'm a gypsy"—his choice of words. He looked like he had lived a tough life and went on, "It's not easy, living in a caravan." It wasn't hard to believe.

"How much do you drink?"

"I used to be a heavy drinker, about seven or eight pints a night. It's less now."

He told me he had smoked since the age of ten, an average of thirty per day or seventy-five pack years—a phenomenal amount. He had chronic obstructive airway disease and there was no way he was fit for a transplant. Patrick told me he had pain in his legs with walking, due to blocked arteries in his legs, which suggested to me that other major arteries would be clogged with atheroma, putting him at high risk of having a heart attack or a stroke.

I broke the news to him. The myelofibrosis CNS sat at the back of the room, looking sympathetic. "Patrick, although your myelofibrosis is severe enough to consider a transplant, it isn't the right treatment for you. It would be too risky, with maybe a 50% chance that you wouldn't survive."

Patrick was not surprised or disappointed, as being confined to a hospital room for weeks would have been very strange to him. I decided to spend the rest of the consultation planning how to address his other medical problems. I asked about his family support.

"I live alone, but I have five children," from four different women, two of them Romany. He was in contact with all of them, and they all lived in Somerset.

"Patrick, I suggest that you continue to see your specialist about your myelofibrosis. You may need blood transfusions at some point. Keep your appointments with the lung clinic and try to stop smoking. I realise how hard it is." Patrick said he would try hypnotherapy, and mushroom extracts for his enlarged spleen. I had no problem with the mushrooms, but also wanted him to pursue conventional therapy. "Go to your GP and get referred about the pain in the legs. I think you have narrowing of the major leg arteries, which can be dealt with by a surgeon or a radiologist."

He was grateful and relieved and thanked me for my advice. A transplant would have shortened his life as he wasn't well enough to have the procedure. Patrick continues to battle with all his medical problems and survives without much help.

Russell was a balding, red-faced, somewhat overweight accountant, who never exercised. He was diagnosed with AML, totally out of the blue. He worried about everything, with good reason, as it turned out.

We gave him standard aggressive therapy for a middle-aged man. It didn't work at all. A month later, he still had 90% blasts in his marrow, slightly more than when we had started. He had had a rough time with fevers and weight loss and was in hospital continuously. I gave him the marrow result.

"Russ, it hasn't worked. We need to move on to our salvage regimen, called FLAG-Ida. That has about a 40% chance of getting remission. If we can get remission, we may need to do a transplant." Russ lived alone but had a supportive family.

"Forty per cent? Is that all?"

I nodded. I liked him, and there was no beating around the bush. He wanted the unvarnished truth.

"Would you have this salvage treatment?" he asked. Some patients worry about asking their doctor what they would do, but actually, it's a smart question.

"Yes, I would. It has a real chance of working. You are still curable, and we shouldn't give up now. It will be hard, and I think you will have to spend another four weeks in hospital."

"OK, doc. When can we start?"

"Tomorrow. We will know the outcome in about four weeks."

The chemo was really tough. He had no white cells and experienced continual fevers, requiring antibiotics and antifungal drugs. The counts didn't recover, which is a bad sign. "We should do a marrow to see where you are," I told him. "It could show obvious leukaemia, which would be bad, or it could be empty, which might mean we will need to repeat it in a week or so."

"What do you think it will show?" he asked, a question most patients don't have the courage for.

"I don't know, but I am a bit concerned about the lack of count recovery. I will tell you the result first thing tomorrow."

The marrow was quite sparse but there were lots of immature (blast-like) cells. Normally, we would have confirmed this was leukaemia by doing flow cytometry, but this didn't work with his form of leukaemia. The marrow was seen by three expert morphologists, who agreed that the marrow showed residual leukaemia. I had a look at the marrow, but don't have the expertise to contradict colleagues who specialise in morphology. I wasn't looking forward to telling him the bad news.

"Russ, I am sorry. There's still a lot of leukaemia there. There's no obvious third-line therapy, but we could look for an experimental treatment if you like. You might need to transfer your care to Birmingham or Oxford."

"I want to go home. Can I go home now?"

I nodded, adding that we would arrange palliative care to contact him and that he could come in for transfusions twice a week if he wished. "How long will it be?"

It would likely be only a few days to a few weeks before the leukaemia caught up with him, and I told him so. He went home that afternoon, and we arranged for our CNS to call him twice a week. I was away on holiday for two weeks and handed him over to a colleague. Russ reported feeling OK and said he was going for short walks with his brother, who had moved in with him. He was offered an appointment in the day unit but preferred to stay at home. About two weeks later, he emailed me, to say that he felt quite good ('I thought I would be dead by now').

I brought him in for a blood count, which showed everything in the normal range. We followed up with a marrow. The marrow was completely different to the last time. It was cellular and healthy. He was in remission, demonstrating that the immature cells my colleagues had seen were not leukaemia cells after all, but recovering early cells.

"Russ, we were wrong when we told you that there was still leukaemia, it was just recovering cells. This is very unusual, but I think you may be ok. You're probably really cross with us."

"Not at all. What do we do now?" I explained that he should probably have some more chemo but then we would stop and see what happened. Russ had been given his life back.

## Amoli

Amoli, a very good-looking man who regularly went to the gym, was too busy to be ill. He was a cardiology and emergency department consultant, who was working sixty hours a week, despite having Crohn's disease, a gut problem that required lots of therapy including low-dose chemotherapy, used as an immune suppressant. This caused him to develop secondary leukaemia with a bad prognosis due to a chromosome abnormality. He needed a transplant.

136

Amoli was of Indian origin, but fortunately, he had a matched sibling who could donate stem cells. We were very worried that the transplant would affect his bowels, and it was even possible that the bowel could be perforated during the transplant. Everybody gets an inflamed gut during a transplant, a condition called mucositis.

Amoli liked facts. "What's my chance of cure?"

"About 20–25%." He didn't blink, he was expecting this.

"What's my chance of dying of the transplant?" He got there first.

"About 20%, but I can't be sure given your Crohn's disease, even though it's inactive. It probably increases the risk of dying."

"How long will I need off work?"

"Given the stresses of your job, and the undesirability of you coming into contact with patients with viral infections, I am going to say six months. If you can do some work from home, you might be able to go back part-time for about four months."

He grimaced; being unable to work did not sound attractive.

"I don't think you should be too hard on yourself. You will feel tired when you restart work. If you get chronic GVHD, you will need longer off work, and if it's very bad you might need to change your job."

Amoli sailed through the transplant, going home after around two weeks. 'I told you David'. His bowels withstood the chemotherapy, and I told him to feel free to break all records. He smiled.

I saw him every two weeks in outpatients, but he was so well that he barely needed a doctor. "Do I need to come and see you this often?"

"Yes."

We did bone marrow biopsies at one, three and twelve months, which were all clear. We managed to get the full results to him within one week, waiting for the outcome of the marrows made him anxious.

He went back to work at four months, initially part-time. He told me he was bored at home and was back to exercising so he couldn't see why he should delay his return to work any longer. He did get some infections, but none of them serious.

Amoli got very minor skin GVHD, treated with steroid cream. His Crohn's disease has stayed inactive, the transplant probably helped with that too! (Transplant is a recognised therapy for severe Crohn's disease.)

I did another marrow at twenty-four months (again normal), and we agreed that from there on we would follow his disease by blood counts.

"Do you think I am cured?" he asked.

"You have a good chance. If you get to five years, I will be pretty confident." Amoli didn't always attend yearly follow-ups but preferred to send an email saying he was really well, his blood counts were normal and he was too busy to take half a day off.

Then, quite recently, out of the blue, I got a call from Amoli.

"Hi, are you OK?"

"Yes, I'm fine. Today is ten years from my transplant. My blood count last week was normal, and I am working harder than ever. I just wanted to remind you of this milestone and thank you again."

"Amoli, you've made my day! Stay well, and don't work too hard!" He laughed.

"I can't promise that."

## An unfortunate life

Robert had not had a normal life; his multiple encounters with cancer had seen to that. He was the only child in a middle-class professional family. His mother was forty when she had him. After fifteen years of trying, they were delighted with their baby.

All was well until he was three when he was diagnosed with ALL. In 2022, his chance of cure would have been over 90% but thirty years ago he probably had only a 50/50 chance. He had the usual UK national trial chemotherapy for about three years, and at five years from diagnosis (at the age of eight) the paediatrician treating him said he was likely to be cured. He was doing well at school (despite an interrupted education); all seemed well.

That was when his father left his mother. I met Robert's father many years later, who told me the story from his point of view. Robert's mother totally devoted herself to her child with leukaemia and wasn't able to give her husband much attention. With time, he found a new partner and decided to leave when his son was pronounced cured, feeling he had done his duty. He remained in touch with his son.

This devastated Robert's mother, who devoted even more time to Robert. This wasn't good for Robert, who didn't have many friends at school. They almost never came home with him, and he had few playdates. He was different, partly because he had spent too much time in hospitals, or with his mum; schoolkids can be quite unforgiving when they sense difference. Nevertheless, Robert did well at school and got into a good London university to study Economics.

He was in a six-person apartment in a hall of residence that included two girls. He was interested in girls but had never had a girlfriend. He lacked the social confidence to ask girls out, as well as being short, in unfashionable clothes and with a dorky haircut.

At the age of nineteen, he noticed some discomfort in his right testicle while cycling. He was having yearly follow-ups for his leukaemia; his oncologist thought it might be recurrent ALL. It wasn't: it was a new primary tumour of the testis (a teratoma). This was also curable. He had the testicle removed and then received six months of intensive, debilitating chemotherapy.

His chance of cure was very high: with ALL this is one of the big success stories of modern oncology. He deferred his studies for a year, then completed his degree. Two cancers before the age of twenty: Robert was seriously unlucky but lived to fight another day.

After university he got a good job in finance in Bristol, continuing to live with his mum. His confidence was further dented by the operation, he didn't feel attractive to women and dreaded having to reveal his cancer history and the possibility of being sub-fertile. At the age of thirty-five, he presented to his GP with a mass over his upper jaw. This was biopsied by a facio-maxillary surgeon and found to be leukaemia. It was not his ALL, but AML, presumably secondary to his two previous malignancies and their treatment.

He was treated with chemotherapy again, not the same as his ALL treatment, and the facial mass went away. At this point, Robert was referred to me for a transplant. It was clearly his best option, but it only had a 30% chance of cure. Worse than that, I had to tell him that doing a transplant would increase his chance of getting another cancer, as well as making him infertile. We collected his semen and although the sperm analysis wasn't normal, there was hope of him conceiving through IVF.

Robert and his mum sat close, almost too close together in the small clinic room. They were made of tough stuff; they had heard it all before. There was a 25% chance of dying of the transplant and only a modest chance of cure, but I strongly recommended that we went ahead. There is a personal element in the decision-making, but they realised the recommendation was the unanimous view of all the leukaemia consultants and accepted the advice. Robert was in the hospital for five weeks.

The nurses loved him. He never complained, did exactly what they asked and always found the energy to ask them how they were feeling. 'He is such a sweet man, especially when you consider what he has gone through' was one comment. Each patient is assigned their own nurse to provide continuity of care, and his was called Annette. Annette was short with plain brown hair tied back in a ponytail.

She radiated warmth and always seemed to be smiling. They had long chats, and she confided to him that she also had ALL as a child (a history not uncommon in transplant nurses). She helped him with his concerns but often stayed in the room longer when she had time, just to chat. She was working on the day he went home and asked for his email address so she could check he was alright. He didn't have the courage to ask for hers.

Robert did well, and the leukaemia stayed in remission. Annette repeatedly asked me about his progress but also emailed him once a month. Another nurse told me that Annette 'fancied' Robert, but I didn't feel I could intervene. Robert looked forward to Annette's emails. One day about twelve months after the transplant, he received an email from Annette. It said, "Robert, it has been a while since I looked after you. I wonder if you would like to meet up. Perhaps we could go for a coffee?"

## 'Looks like a good game'

It was September in Melbourne, the time of the football finals. My Australian rules football team Hawthorn, the team I had supported since the age of five, was playing. I was twenty-three, a second-year doctor, doing a very busy cardiology rotation, and didn't know if I would be working the weekend until quite close to the match, so I hadn't bought a ticket. When I tried to, the game was sold out, and I went to the ground to buy a ticket from a scalper, (technically, it was illegal if the price was higher than the ticket's original price).

Near one of the entrances, I saw a middle-aged man holding up a couple of tickets. "Hi, how much? Where is it?" He had a red face, greying hair and was a bit overweight. It was a sunny, early autumn day, with a gentle breeze, perfect for football.

"It'll cost you thirty dollars, which is what I bought it for. It's on the wing, five rows back from the front, with an unobstructed view," he told me.

"Great! Here's thirty dollars." He gave me a ticket.

"My son couldn't come at the last moment, so you'll be sitting next to me." He looked at my scarf and said, "Good to see you are a Hawk supporter. We'll get on just fine!"

We walked towards the turnstile, and he went through first. It was crowded; the match was due to start in fifteen minutes; and we paused before going down some steps. Suddenly, he turned round to look at me. He went white and had a frightened look on his face. He sank to the ground and then rolled onto his back. I put my finger on his carotid pulse. He was not breathing.

I pulled open his shirt and shouted, "This man has had a cardiac arrest! I am going to resuscitate him. Clear some space!"

Everyone around us immediately gave me room. A policeman arrived with a walkie-talkie, and I told him to call an ambulance and get St John's first here, so they can help me. In fact, two St John's first aiders arrived almost immediately and helped with his breathing with a mask and breathing bag, while the other called the ambulance.

"He needs to be shocked. Is there a defibrillator?"

I did this all the time in my cardiology rotation, and I was on for cardiac arrests around the hospital, of which there were two or three each day. The two MICA ambulance men arrived while I was still manually compressing his chest, with a substantial crowd encircling us. The ambulance crew arrived and zapped him: no response, no cardiac output. The second time, they were able to detect a pulse and the ECG showed he was back in sinus rhythm. He woke up, opened his eyes and started to breathe by himself.

Some of the crowd started clapping. One of the ambulance men said, "We're going to take him to the Alfred. I think he's going to do fine."

I explained I was a junior doctor, doing my cardiology rotation, and that I had just bought a football ticket from him.

"Well, it's his lucky day. Timing is everything. You should watch the footy. Looks like a good game."

I took his name and then went upstairs to the seat which had an empty space next to it. It was also my lucky day: our team won and when I rang later, the Alfred coronary care nurse said "He's OK. It looks like an inferior infarct, no more arrhythmias." A few weeks later he sent me a lovely thank you card. We stayed in touch for the next two years, and he was well and didn't require heart surgery (this was before coronary angioplasty was routinely performed). It was so nice to do something unequivocally useful, as well as have a good story to tell at dinner parties.

I will contrast this experience with a more recent episode. Most Sundays I ride with my local cycling club on well-organised rides of 50–80 km. The routes are planned and the rides are led by people trained in first aid. I join the level three rides, which is the lowest level, but in fact, everybody on those rides is a good cyclist.

I was away overseas so I missed a ride that had only six people. One of them was Patrick, a fit seventy-two-year-old. They were halfway through the ride, riding in three pairs when he swerved out onto the wrong side of the road, narrowly missing a car then to the left, into a hedge. One of the following riders screamed and everybody stopped. He was unconscious, wrapped around the bike, with his arms through the frame.

They were worried about moving him but carefully removed him from the bike and started resuscitation. Two people were trained and shared duties. A first responder arrived in his car in eight minutes and took over. His ECG was flat (this is called an asystolic arrest, it has a very poor outcome); he tried some adrenaline, but it didn't work. The air ambulance arrived soon after, they tried various manoeuvres, but it didn't work, he died in the middle of the countryside. I felt a bit guilty that I was not there but actually, I was able to reassure the leader of the ride, that it would have made no difference.

# Chapter 9
# The Bizarre and the Inexplicable

### An unfortunate series of events

One of my leukaemia patients was three years from diagnosis, in remission and back at work, doing normal things—or so it seemed. I was seeing him briefly every four months in the clinic. He invariably had normal blood counts and no complaints; he would smile when I enquired about his family. His wife was lovely and supportive, was always there during his treatment but was now devoting her efforts to their two young boys, and her job. She hadn't noticed a change in his mood.

One Friday, his wife and kids headed off to spend the weekend with her parents in the Wirral. It was a long drive: his wife picked the kids up straight from school and set off. Ray did an ordinary day's work, mainly tidying up a few cases at his law firm, sending summaries to his team of where he had got to. At about 9:00 pm that night, he was in the emergency room, on a trolley, in great pain in the heels of both feet. A&E was full, there was barely room for the trolley.

He was seen by a quite junior doctor, who did plain X-rays and found a linear (hairline) undisplaced fracture in the left calcaneus (heel bone). He was given crutches and pain relief, told to not bear weight for two weeks and given an appointment for a fracture clinic. Apart from establishing that it occurred after a fall, nobody had asked him exactly how it happened. A and E were busy that night.

Two weeks later, he was sitting in a small room in the fracture clinic, across the desk from an orthopaedic registrar, who also was in a hurry. "Your right heel is also fractured, they missed it," he was told. Ray was given some general advice about rest and not injuring himself further and prescribed some more analgesics. As Ray was literally walking out the door, the registrar asked, "By the way, how did you do this?"

He seemed really flat.

Ray sat down again. He was relieved to be asked. He had tied a rope to a beam in the tallest room in his house, carefully fitted a noose around his neck and then stepped off a chair about three feet off the ground. The noose tightened. He had a dreadful feeling of uncertainty, that he had made a mistake. Then the rope broke, and he hit the floor, with considerable force.

The orthopaedic registrar visibly grimaced. He was so far behind on his scheduled list and his consultant would criticise him for taking too much time over people with 'simple' fractures. "I am going to refer you to psychiatry," he said to Ray. "They may want to admit you. Can you wait outside? The clinic nurse will check in on you."

"Liz, can you keep an eye on this guy, his fall was actually a suicide attempt, make sure he stays to be seen by psych."

The young, friendly enthusiastic psych reg arrived fifteen minutes later, took a brief psychiatric history, called her consultant and told Ray, "Amazingly, we have a bed in our unit, and you need to come in. We think you have some features of recurrent unipolar depression. The standard treatment is lithium, but we have a trial comparing this with a similar drug, which has the same side effects but might be more effective."

Ray agreed to go on the trial (after asking his wife's opinion) and was randomised to the experimental agent. This caused him to pass urine all day and all night. He couldn't stop drinking and was referred to the kidney specialists, who diagnosed nephrogenic diabetes insipidus, a condition in which the kidney doesn't respond normally to the hormone that allows us to pass concentrated urine (antidiuretic hormone).

"We are studying this condition and correlating it with changes in the renal tubules: we would like to do a kidney biopsy. This is a low-risk procedure and it will show if you have any other kidney problems," Ray was told. The vast majority of kidney biopsies pass without incident, but Ray was unlucky. The biopsy needle hit major blood vessels in the kidney and caused an abnormal connection between an artery and a vein called a fistula. This bled; he needed to be transfused several units of blood and spent some time in the high-dependency unit of intensive care so he could be carefully monitored. Meanwhile, he was getting steadily more depressed.

The best way of stopping the bleeding was for a radiologist to close the abnormal arterio-venous connection by squirting some glue-like fluid into the fistula. Unfortunately, the glue flowed backwards into the aorta and then into the blood vessels that supply the bowel. The blood supply to most of his small bowel was cut off. It became necrotic and Ray didn't survive the operation that tried to remove the dead bowel. He had wanted to die, but not in this cruel, prolonged and painful way.

The coroner became involved and deemed the cause of death a medical misadventure. It was hard to know where to point the finger. Both his wife and I had missed his depression, but most of the things that happened were just an unfortunate series of events.

## Inexplicable behaviour

I think that, in some respects, I may have been regarded as a rather staid and serious young man, too focused on school, university work and my career. However, I always had lots of other interests and was quite sporty. I was a very quick runner (I got that from my father, who was a sprinter, and my mother, who was a good long jumper). My mother loved houses, and we moved every four or five years.

From one of our houses in Melbourne, it took three tram rides to get to school. Transferring from one tram to another efficiently was key to arriving on time, as arriving late was not tolerated: you would get a detention and if it recurred, the school would write to your parents.

To liven up the journey, we 'tram-hopped'. I will explain. Trams are huge electric vehicles on rails that are the mainstay of the public transport system in Melbourne, like Lisbon and San Francisco. From the centre of the city of Melbourne, you needed to take the number eight tram to Melbourne Grammar School (MGS). However, these trams were infrequent, so it was best to take any tram going down St Kilda Road, the main road out of the city.

When trams stopped at traffic lights or at tram stops, we would dash, in our distinctive school uniform with our book-laden school bags, to the tram ahead. We didn't always make it and commonly jumped onto a moving tram or had to re-catch the tram we were on. The tram drivers and conductors hated this game but were powerless to stop it. People were always running for trams in Melbourne—it was a city in a hurry. This was somewhat dangerous but not particularly unusual for MGS pupils, so one day my schoolmates and I thought of a new dare.

The two-rail tram tracks on the other side of the road ran quite close but there was a small gap between the two trams and their running boards where you would step off the tram. The dare was to stand precisely in the middle of the road and have trams pass on either side of you simultaneously.

"I'm going to do it." My mates looked at each other excitedly, then realised I was serious.

"Marksy, don't do it. It's fucking dangerous. If you get it wrong, you'll die," one of my friends warned.

"There's definitely enough space. All I have to do is stand in the exact middle and I'll be fine."

I didn't want to overthink it. I got off the tram, went round the back and stood in the space between the two tram tracks just before the tram arrived, travelling in the opposite direction. I stood side-on, to occupy as little space as possible, and closed my eyes. In those days, I was quite thin. I could feel the 'whoosh' the two trams created as they passed. My schoolmates watched on in horror.

I'm sure I traumatised the tram drivers: they had not expected this and there wasn't time to stop. Having passed me on either side, they stopped their trams, got out of their cabins and yelled at me (quite justifiably). "What in the hell were you doing? Melbourne Grammar! Bloody typical, we'll report you!" (although to my knowledge, they didn't).

My school friends watched this in awe. I was stupid, but I was also a genius: this feat would not be replicated. The tale of my exploit spread widely around the school, and a number of people came up to me to talk about it. It was really dumb, and I don't know why I did it. I told everyone not to tell my brothers so that my mother (who would have been furious) didn't find out. I look back at this and can scarcely believe I did it: it was so out of character for me as a fourteen-year-old.

## A real pain

I was there when Tyler first arrived at the hospital with ALL. He had terrible pain all over: he couldn't localise it or tell us where it hurt most. All the marrow cavities of his long bones were stuffed full of leukaemic cells, growing rapidly, causing a deep, throbbing, bony discomfort. His legs hurt, his arms hurt and when he rolled over his ribs hurt. It was excruciating when he coughed.

Ten out of ten pain; he didn't know what to do with himself. We gave him 10 mg of morphine, which produced a marked improvement, and he drifted off to sleep. He knew he had ALL and had been told that he had an 80% chance of cure. We did a bone marrow biopsy (that also hurt) and started him on regular steroids to reduce the pain.

Tyler was twenty, of average height, with a mop of purple-stained hair, and piercings in his lip and ear. He was good-looking in a raffish kind of way and had an impudent smile. He spoke with an exaggerated south London accent, every phrase beginning with 'like': even at the onset of a potentially fatal condition, he wanted to sound like a real geezer. From the start, I quite liked him, but I knew he would be hard work. Tyler's girlfriend had beautiful blond hair and was extremely thin. Both of them had lots of visible tattoos, including skull bones on their knuckles.

His well-dressed American mum was not allowed in the room generally, but I insisted that she join Tyler and Hannah when I spoke to them about his leukaemia. Tyler and his mum moved to the UK when her marriage ended, and she had met a British man who lived in Bristol. Tyler, without any effort, got good grades at school, good enough to get an offer to do History at Durham. He dropped out early in his second year, having been asked to leave for reasons that were not apparent. I thought it very likely that he used drugs, but he denied this, other than a bit of weed before he dropped out of university.

Tyler spent the whole four weeks of induction in the hospital. This was unusual because he sailed into remission and had no fevers. We couldn't discharge him, however, because of the pain he was in: nine or ten out of ten pain, all over. This wasn't due to leukaemia anymore because the leukaemic cells were nearly all gone. On day 29, his marrow showed a deep molecular remission.

His mum was angry with us. "When are you going to fix his pain? I think some of the staff don't believe he has pain."

When a patient with cancer says they have pain, our first instinct is always to believe them: they have real pain until proven otherwise. Tyler's description of his pain was vague. Tyler was unable to describe the pain, saying "It just hurts, prof." We got palliative and supportive care involved, who were similarly puzzled. They tried different opiate drugs including fentanyl patches, but he continued to say he had pain, and we were unable to wean him off analgesics. At the time of evaluating him for pain, he had small pupils and a low heart rate, and he did not appear to be in distress.

Tyler was given various oral painkilling drugs but said they didn't work. We later found out that he didn't take most of them: he pretended to swallow them,

147

then took them out of his mouth and stored them in his bedside cabinet for later use. I was suspicious: something wasn't right. I spoke to him about his leukaemia but all he wanted to talk about was pain relief. Sometimes he wasn't in his room; he would disappear to smoke outside and be gone for hours. Some of the nurses on the ward would see him meeting with friends, just up the road from the oncology centre.

Three months after diagnosis, it was clear he was addicted to opiates and there was no plausible reason for his all-over body pain. I spoke with the palliative care consultant, who agreed and suggested that we both discuss the issue with Tyler, telling him that we would be withdrawing him from these drugs and that this would be difficult for him. We saw him alone.

He was defensive, and a bit aggressive. "Just because you can't work out the cause of my pain doesn't mean I haven't got it."

"We are not saying that. But we are arranging for you to come off these drugs because they don't work and they are only doing you harm. We will start you on some different pain-modifying drugs and see how you go."

We started him on an antidepressant, which helped very much. Eventually, we got him off the drugs, and he remains well to this day. Quite a lot of patients with leukaemia have torrid beginnings to their treatment but are fine after they have got through the first few months.

## The violent patient

Very few patients attack their doctors. Most of the time, they realise we are doing our best to help them. Even when things go wrong, it's not usually our fault. Apparently, nurses are more commonly the victims of aggression, particularly in A&E from confused patients. So, when patients or their families express violent thoughts towards us, it comes as a surprise. Sometimes, there is no warning.

You may be in a small room with a person who may be far physically stronger than you. There is nowhere to run, and there are lots of objects they can use to harm you. Most patients who attack doctors have psychiatric histories or personality disorders. In my entire career, I have only had a few patients threaten me. My practice is to immediately find a chaperone. I then explain to the patient that I can no longer look after them and that their care will be transferred to somebody else.

Jim just couldn't accept his diagnosis. He couldn't believe he had cancer, and he certainly didn't believe that he deserved this diagnosis. So, he blamed his doctor (me).

"Are you sure about the diagnosis?"

"Yes. The biopsy has been looked at by three pathologists, who all agree that it is cancer. We discuss each patient in a multidisciplinary team meeting and come to a consensus. The clinicians who look after patients also review the biopsy in our weekly meeting. It's clear-cut." He looked at me as if he was considering killing me.

"It's your fault, Professor Marks. I didn't do anything wrong."

"Most patients with leukaemia haven't done anything wrong. We don't understand why most people develop cancer." He scowled at me. "What we need to do is accept this situation and work out what we are going to do about it. There may be a chance of curing you." My petite CNS arrived in the room.

"Hello, Jim, sorry I am late. I was with another patient. I couldn't leave; he had just received bad news."

Jim wasn't impressed. He went red in the face, looked like he was going to explode. Eventually, he screamed, "Fucking hell!" and stormed out of the room. The CNS and I looked at each other in disbelief. I said, "I shouldn't say this, but I really don't like him. I think he might actually hit me. No patient has ever done that."

"He makes me feel unsafe," agreed the CNS.

"Can you call him later? I think he has a partner, God help her. Can you try to get them both on the line together?"

"I'll try."

I spoke to the CNS the next day.

"How did it go?"

"Terrible. He kept talking over me. His partner Jude didn't say anything. I wouldn't be surprised if he abused her. He said some really worrying things, like 'death and suffering are the wages of sin' and 'I am going to take him down' and 'I will slit his throat'. He blames you."

"Right. We will report this, and I will need you to repeat exactly what he said. We should get the police involved. You have to treat these threats seriously. He could be waiting outside the hospital. He might even follow me home." I contacted the general manager and said I never wanted to see this patient again. The GM agreed but said I had a duty to find him another doctor.

"I disagree," I said. "That's his problem. Staff safety first. He lost his rights when he talked about slitting my throat. When and if he finds another doctor, I will send the notes and communicate with them, but I am not going to actively pass a violent patient onto another doctor."

She knew I wouldn't budge from this. I had been the chair of the ethics committee at my college for five years. I was on firm ground. "I will, on the other hand, speak to his GP and ask them to refer him to a psychiatrist. I think he has a severe personality disorder and it would be useful to make that diagnosis."

The GP, when I spoke to him, said that due to his behaviour, they had been close on several occasions to excluding him from the surgery. He referred Jim to psychiatry but, of course, could not compel him to attend. He tried to soften the blow by suggesting that the psychiatrist hoped to help him with the stress of the new diagnosis.

Jim didn't darken the doors of our hospital again and died rapidly of his leukaemia, having refused to accept this diagnosis or any treatment; this is most unusual. I felt sorry for his partner.

Doctors and nurses are doing their best, and we really care about what happens to our patients. We don't deserve to be physically threatened.

## She just wouldn't die

Bone marrow transplanters deal with a lot of dying patients, so we should be good at identifying people who are on the way out. It isn't always easy. When in doubt, we talk to our colleagues or a palliative care specialist; when you have looked after a patient for five years or more you aren't always objective about changes in their clinical status. Raelene was one such person. She was very bright and full of life, thirty-nine years old, with two teenage children and a devoted husband, although I didn't see him in the hospital much because he was looking after the kids.

She had a high-powered job in banking and continued to work through the early stages of her AML treatment. She had high-risk AML and needed a transplant to have a reasonable chance of a cure. She agreed to go into a randomised trial comparing two pre-transplant chemotherapy conditioning regimens and drew the arm that included very strong chemotherapy.

The transplant was a disaster from the beginning; she just didn't tolerate the chemotherapy. If you gave this high-dose chemo to a hundred people, everybody would have side effects; a small number of severe side effects; and maybe two people would become life-threateningly ill. Some patients are more sensitive for reasons that are not clear. Chemotherapy before a transplant is designed to kill the maximum number of leukaemia cells but leave the normal organs in the body able to recover, even though they may take a hit. About a week after the chemotherapy, her skin became red and inflamed.

She developed terrible diarrhoea and abdominal pain due to severe damage to her gut lining (mucositis). She became gravely ill, requiring two intensive care admissions due to loss of fluid and infection, causing low blood pressure. ITU was full of COVID cases at the time, and she had to wait hours for a bed to become available. These delays put our ward under enormous pressure because she needed one-on-one nursing, as well as weakening her greatly. Her blood counts improved when the graft 'took' and she rallied, but then she got a life-threatening GVHD of the gut.

This resulted in more diarrhoea and more abdominal pain. She started to pass blood, and we kept adding therapies because none of them worked. We kept going, but she continued to pass two litres of stool a day and became unable to control it. She was embarrassed by these episodes of incontinence and apologised (unnecessarily) to the nursing staff.

As my week as an attending consultant on the ward started, she was fading. I reviewed her treatment and admitted to her (and her husband) that nothing had worked. There were still some things we could try, but they had almost no chance of working, and Raelene and her husband decided to stop all active treatment. The palliative care nurse strongly agreed, and we withdrew everything but medication to keep her comfortable.

I left on Thursday, thinking she would die over the weekend. Her children came in to see her and said goodbye. They took a selfie with her. Her husband offered to show the photo to me, but I couldn't bear to look at it. I made an excuse.

On Monday, she was still alive. The diarrhoea had stopped. I have seen this happen: opiates stop the bowel contracting but don't help the underlying problem. She woke up and asked to see the children. Her husband was anxious not to confuse the kids by giving them ambiguous messages.

He said to a nurse, "Surely, the doctors can get this right?"

This situation, in which treatment is withdrawn and the patient expects death to follow rapidly, is not infrequent. Some patients are so strong that their body refuses to give up: they just won't die.

Raelene did die eventually, two weeks later, in her sleep. We felt guilty about being so relieved.

### 'They wake me up on Tuesdays'

It was Wednesday, the second of three consultant ward rounds that occurred every week. The ward was really busy and doing a full round was a painstaking, exhausting affair. We left Annette towards the end of the round. Only the BMT patient with COVID remained: we had to see this patient last for infection control reasons. The registrar and more junior doctors were looking up results and making phone calls, so I said I would see her on my own.

Annette had been in the hospital for nearly six weeks despite having no major complications after her transplant. When I entered the room, she was lying in bed, eyes half-closed, occasionally groaning. She wouldn't get out of bed and wasn't eating. We put in a nasogastric tube to feed her, but it kept on coming out. We said she could eat anything she liked, even food we normally did not allow, to no avail.

Annette said she wasn't hungry. She was thin, with grey, unkempt hair and wore drab hospital pyjamas. Many patients rebel against this clothing: they don't want to look like this, but Annette didn't care. Physios and occupational therapists came to her room to help her walk, to at least get her sitting out of bed. She would do the walking but none of the extra exercises they suggested.

I asked some screening questions to work out if she was depressed, but she interrupted me, saying, "I'm not depressed. I'm just completely exhausted."

Patients don't always recognise that their mood is low, however, so we brought in a psychiatrist. The young, smiling psych registrar felt that she was not significantly depressed, but she did have some symptoms of anxiety.

"You might want to try some diazepam," he suggested.

"I will, but I'm worried about causing further side effects," and he agreed that this was a risk. Try as we might, there was overwhelming negativity about her from the staff. Her nurse described her as a 'heart sink' and said over a ten-hour shift that he couldn't get her to do anything he asked. Of course, you shouldn't talk about a patient this way, but doctors and nurses are human too. We sometimes despair about the task ahead of us. Her nurse told me, "I don't think she's depressed. I think she's had a mental breakdown."

I was due to see her on my own, but I really wasn't certain that I could turn things around.

"Hi Annette, it's Professor Marks, how are you doing today?"

"OK," was the brief answer.

"You look a bit tired," I observed. "Are you sleeping properly?"

"No. I keep getting woken up at night."

"Do you mean by the nurses? They have to do obs [observations] every four hours."

Annette told me that the nurses were waking her every two hours, and seemed to have a paranoid belief that they were waking her out of spite. In fact, nurses rotating onto night duty are tired themselves and just want to safely get through the night, hand over to the day shift, and go home to sleep. They hate waking sleeping patients because they realise how hard it is to sleep in the hospital. Suddenly, I realised something was wrong. She wasn't registering the reasons behind my questions and wasn't responding properly.

Finally, she spoke. She looked up at me earnestly and said, "They wake me up on Tuesdays."

What did she mean?

She spoke again, this time more emphatically. "They 'wake' me up on Tuesdays."

I tried to test her orientation to time and place, but she would only say this same sentence, maybe twenty times. We call this perseveration and it may be a sign of damage to the frontal lobes of the brain. The following day she was better, but could not recall the conversation we had had.

She said, "I think I'm losing my mind."

I was inclined to agree with her. Bone marrow transplants are amongst the toughest procedures NHS patients face. Haematologists administer potentially lethal doses of chemotherapy and radiotherapy to kill the maximum number of leukaemic cells. These drugs can affect any organ in the body, including the brain, although that is less common.

This procedure was just too much for Annette; she didn't have enough reserve organ function to withstand the stresses of the procedure. Sometimes, you don't know this until you do the transplant. We carefully assess every transplant patient to see if they are strong enough to withstand the procedure, but sometimes we get it wrong.

Annette did not survive. She did get home via a hospital rehab ward but never regained her strength and died about four months after the transplant. I later found out that they assigned a different nurse to her every day because nobody was robust enough to look after her multiple days in a row. We discussed her at a morbidity and mortality review meeting.

Some said that it was reasonable to proceed with the transplant as it gave her a chance of cure, but I very much regretted doing the transplant. We did Annette no favours: we didn't extend her life and there was no quality. Looking after Annette was a big stress for the staff many of whom said that Annette had 'worn them out'. Annette's story, even though I had a small part in it, made me feel sad.

## Serial sevens

Doctors have several ways of assessing patients' cognitive function to see whether their brain is functioning normally. We test their orientation to time, place and person. We ask them what day and month it is, who is the Prime Minister etc. Some acutely confused patients are unable to answer those questions satisfactorily and can be frightened when they realise they are getting the answers wrong.

If they get the answers right, we look in more depth at how their brain is processing data. 'Serial sevens' is an exercise in which we ask a patient to subtract seven from 100 (93), then another seven (86), then another (79) and so on. Patients hate being put on the spot, even when their brains are functioning normally; some are unable to do this under pressure. The arithmetic is easy for most people, the problem is remembering the last number.

Rachel was the last person I would have expected to have trouble with this assessment. She had just finished a maths degree at Oxford and was about to study medicine. She was twenty, delightfully mature and friendly. She had a rare cancer (acute myelofibrosis) that needed a transplant. The procedure went well, but then she relapsed about a year later.

Unusually, I decided to do a second transplant, with a different donor. Second transplants are hard; they have more complications and a higher chance of mortality. One such complication is thrombotic thrombocytopenic purpura (TTP), where small clots in blood vessels compromise the blood supply to organs such as the brain and kidneys.

About two weeks after the transplant, as I arrived in the ward one of the senior nurses literally grabbed hold of me. "David, could you see Rachel first?" This was surprising, as we normally see the most ill patients first.

"Why? She was doing OK yesterday."

154

"Her nurse overnight thought she was confused. When I saw her, she was fully oriented, but something isn't right." When a senior transplant nurse says this, you take notice.

I knocked on Rachel's door and entered. "Hi, Rachel. How are you doing?"

"Fine. It seems a bit early for you to come to my room. Is everything ok?" I explained that her nurses wondered if she was a bit confused.

"I'm afraid I am going to have to ask you some annoying questions." Her orientation to time, place and person was normal, but a little slow. "I am going to assess your ability to do serial sevens," I said and explained the exercise. She looked alarmed.

"OK. Seven from a hundred is ninety-three."

"And seven from that?"

"Eighty-eight." Wrong.

"Keep going, please."

'Eighty-two'. Wrong. 'Seventy-seven'. Wrong. She stopped when she saw the look on my face.

"Rachel, this isn't like you. Something's up. Is it OK if get your mum on the phone?"

Her mum answered immediately. "Do you remember this complication called TTP that I mentioned in the pre-transplant chat? It's where the small blood vessels get damaged and little clots form in them, making organs not work properly. It kind of fits with your low platelet count and your kidney function that's just a bit abnormal. We'll stop your ciclosporin and do an MRI scan of the brain. I'll come back later today to talk about the results. Why don't you come in, Mrs Jones, so we can talk?"

I waited for Rachel to ask me if this was serious, but she didn't want to hear the answer and didn't ask. (Sometimes, it's mild, and sometimes, it's life-threatening.)

The scan was normal; we stopped the relevant drugs, and she got better in the next few days. The next time I did serial sevens, her answers were correct and swift. 93,86,79,72,65; I stopped her there.

The second transplant cured her bone marrow cancer, and she is now more than fifteen years out, working as a paediatrician. Many types of brain injury are irreversible; the early detection of her problems by our nurses enabled us to turn this around.

# Chapter 10
# Stories from the End of My Career

## My last inpatient

One more job to do. I could feel it hanging over me. Ragita, a patient with ALL, needed to be told her bone marrow biopsy result, which would determine whether she had any chance of survival, and which was due to come through less than two hours before I retired. I very much doubted that the treatment had worked. We weren't even certain we would go ahead with CAR T-cells when we heard her marrow contained 90% leukaemic cells. Every other treatment had failed or had only a partial effect or was transient at best.

I felt it was my responsibility to tell her the outcome of the CAR T-cells she had received, whether it was good or bad. The timing was unfortunate, but it didn't seem fair to hand this duty over to a colleague. She had waited patiently: the bone marrow biopsy to assess treatment response could only be done four weeks after the infusion of the special genetically modified (CAR T) cells. Her husband was in the room, which seemed ominous.

Previously, she hadn't allowed him to be there: she was 'protecting' him, or thought she was. When I saw her for major reviews or bone marrow results, I asked that she call him and put him on speakerphone, and again she wouldn't permit this. He was a roofer, and she said that she was worried that, if he received bad news, he might fall off a roof, leaving their son without a parent.

Ragita had been diagnosed a year ago with breast cancer, which required surgery and chemotherapy. The chemotherapy resulted in a type of secondary acute leukaemia (ALL) with a very poor prognosis. We had planned to do a curative transplant, but the leukaemia came back too quickly. Leukaemia is a not uncommon outcome of breast cancer treatment; we see a few patients every year with this complication.

A woman battles through one diagnosis only to have to confront another. I waited for the email that the flow cytometry lab promised, but then got impatient and looked up the result on their website. It had just been reported. I went down to the ward to tell her.

When I arrived in the haematology ward, everybody at the workstations looked up at me knowing I had her result. Her nurse, Frances, was there, at the nurse's station. She said, "Prof, her husband has just arrived and is in the room with her." Let's do it. Debbie, the palliative care nurse, also came along, as did one of the more junior doctors to document the discussion. The tiny room was crowded. There was a small bed with a side room containing a shower and a toilet.

We donned plastic gowns and gloves and filed into the room. Ragita was sitting up in bed, with her husband on an uncomfortable plastic chair on the other side of the room. Her round, brown smiling face looked up at me expectantly. I found a chair and sat down. "Ragita, it's good news."

"Good news?" she said. "Really?"

"Yes. We did the marrow this morning, and although your blood counts are low, we got enough cells for it to be an analysable sample. We can't find any evidence of leukaemia." I watched a tear run down her husband's cheek. "It's not a perfect sample but the CAR T-cells have worked. You're in remission."

"I can't believe it. I was expecting bad news."

"I am pleasantly surprised too. Ragita, this has been such a difficult time, but we need to start thinking about what to do next. Although we have got remission, it may not last. If we can do a transplant now, we can potentially cure you. There will be risks but this is a real opportunity. And this is the last chance I will get to talk to you about it. Claire is our senior nursing transplant coordinator, and she will answer all your questions about the transplant. However, to be clear, I do think you can get through the transplant and be cured, but there will be significant risks."

"Prof Marks, just before you go, I want to say one thing. I'm sorry for being such a cow."

"You have been through so much." I had taken off my gown and gloves (the remnants of COVID) and she reached out her hand towards me. I fleetingly touched her hand, giving her fingers a slight squeeze, and we smiled at each other. Then I left the room. I didn't look back.

I had done all that I could in the time I had. After the transplant (which others would perform), her fate would be in the hands of the gods.

## My last clinic patient

Katy had a torrid time, for over two years. She was from Devon, in her early forties, short, slightly overweight, hugely positive and always with a cheeky smile. Katy was also diagnosed with an aggressive lymphoma and treated with six months of standard curative chemotherapy. It was tough treatment.

The lymphoma went into remission, but she became unwell again about two years later, with enlarged lymph nodes and an abnormal blood count. This time, the bone marrow biopsies looked like ALL, a different malignancy, possibly arising from the treatment. With her second cancer, she had to endure even tougher chemotherapy and was referred to me for a transplant. Her best source of donor stem cells was from two cord units; this would be a difficult, prolonged procedure, but I thought she could tolerate it.

We took her through the transplant. It was complicated, and she had to stay in the hospital for about eight weeks. Viruses were the main problem, but she still had symptoms of gut GVHD, and we couldn't wean her off steroids. She remained plump in the face (we call this side effect 'Cushingoid') but she never complained. We then discharged her to our near-hospital accommodation, where she was seen twice a week in her flat with one outpatient appointment every fortnight.

She had some diarrhoea, but it was controlled with oral steroids. The senior nurse visiting her in the near hospital flats came to me to discuss her. She teased me, saying, "For some reason, Katy really likes you, David."

I was a little taken aback and said, "Some patients do!"

Other colleagues in BMT coordination came to my defence, declaring, "They all love you, David!"

When I saw her on the patient clinic virtual platform (called DrDoctor), Katy was sitting on her sofa with her husband. Both of us knew it would be the last time. I told Katy that I had arranged for her to be followed up by a colleague who had a lot of experience with cord blood transplants. This was good news, but she wanted me to look after her. I couldn't pretend it wasn't a critical time in her transplant course: it was.

I tried to lighten things up by telling her that she was my last clinic patient, after thousands of clinics. I wanted to be positive. "Katy, our visiting nurses say that every time they see you, you look stronger. Do you agree?" When I first met Katy and her husband, I told them that I was 'straight' with my patients. They need never worry that things were worse than I said they were or that I was holding information back. The result was that she trusted me: if I said she was improving, I really thought she was.

"Definitely, I'm getting better."

"You have some improving symptoms of gut GVHD, and I can't pretend they haven't been a problem but the general rule with cord transplants is that you get through this severity of GVHD." We worked through her issues, checked her drugs and made a plan. I said, "Do you have any questions for me?"

She shook her head. Her eyes were glistening; she spoke slowly.

"I want to thank you for all you have done for me. I believe I wouldn't be here today if it weren't for you."

"Katy, it has been a pleasure. Stay well, and keep letting us know how you are doing. Rachel will see you next time but soon it will be my successor." She nodded. We clicked on the red 'log off' space on the screen; she disappeared from sight. I had seen my final clinic patient, and I was pleased to leave on a positive note. Katy would need prolonged follow-up, but it was possible that we had cured her leukaemia.


## The autumn of the matriarch

It's hard to write objectively about your mum; indeed, that shouldn't even be the goal. A lot of people of my generation have had difficult relationships with their mothers. In 2010, I travelled from the UK to Australia to see mine.

She was eighty-three and had broken her hip two months previously after a fall from a stepladder. She was unable to get out of her hospital bed. She wasn't actively dying, but the medical situation left her with no quality of life, and she decided she would stop eating and drinking. She summoned my brother and said, "Andrew, it's time for me to die."

Andrew had spent a lot of time looking after her but didn't question her right to decide, even though she was the most important person in his life. All he said was, "OK, we will need to tell your doctors. What about seeing David and Bruce one more time? They'll take a while to get here from the UK. I hope David will be able to get compassionate leave." Bruce was not working; he could come at any time.

Blood tests showed she was going into kidney failure because she was dehydrated from not drinking. She emailed me to ask me if I would like to come because she knew she would die in the next few days; I think she emailed rather than calling because she didn't want to put me on the spot. I dropped everything, got a week of compassionate leave and travelled to Australia the next day. When I entered the room, I looked at her briefly from the doorway but then came closer and gave her a rare kiss on the cheek. "Mum, how do you feel?" It felt a bit medical, a bit impersonal.

"Not great. I'm short of breath—there's probably some fluid in my lungs as a result of not passing urine. I am glad it will all be over soon."

Remarkably, she had a previous diagnosis of lung cancer, with a brain metastasis diagnosed three years previously. This had responded brilliantly to surgery and a simple drug inhibitor taken orally that targeted a mutation of the cancer, controlling the cancer in the lung and brain, without significant side effects. Some simple cancer treatments, although not curative, really work.

"Thanks for coming," she said.

"Well, it was the least I could do."

She looked so grey, so helpless, her mind intact but her body broken. She noticed a tear rolling down my face and said, "It's hard, isn't it?" She was remembering the death of her mother and her sister, also from lung cancer, all of them heavy smokers. I remember her hearing the news about her mother dying on the phone, from the UK. All I could do was nod. Unusually for me, the words wouldn't come out. It was worth coming.

There wasn't much time left so we needed to use it well, to say the things that needed to be said. I had recently sent her a newspaper report of a talk I had given at the American Society of Haematology meeting, and she said, "You really are becoming quite well-known, aren't you?" (I was the chair of the ALL Education session, a real honour indicating true international recognition.) She had always followed my career with interest.

"Yeah, things are going very well."

"Your father would have been very proud."

She had never said this before. I think now of all the things I could and should have asked her about him, and the circumstances of his death. It's too late now. We had a most uneven relationship, and even then, as a very senior professor, there was a divide between us.

160

I was her son, but not her equal. We had lots of disagreements over the years, and at times it had been impossible to speak to her on the phone. If she didn't like what I was saying, she would just hang up. At many times in my life, I think she was proud of me but had a lot of difficulty showing it. But it was different this time: we both felt we should get to the point.

I called my brother Michael: "It won't be long, she has pulmonary oedema [excess fluid on the lungs causing breathlessness]. She's going to need something for it soon."

"I know. I hope it won't be drawn out." Two doctors talking about their medical mum. She would have approved of this rational, unemotional discussion.

The next day, the rest of my family arrive and mill around the bed. My oldest brother John is not there: he hasn't seen my mother for years (they had a long-running dispute; he said hurtful things that she cannot forgive). We ask her to reconsider. She says she doesn't want to see him, but 'he can come to the funeral'.

My mother complains of feeling tight in the chest, so I arrange for a small dose of morphine that has been prescribed by her doctors, in anticipation of her worsening (she was on an end-of-life pathway). I promise her she won't suffer unduly.

We leave her to rest, with only my brother Bruce remaining. I walk along Chapel Street in South Yarra, looking in the shop windows, not sure how to fill the time. Bruce calls me about two hours later, saying, "She's gone." We all return to the bedside, relieved that the end was quick. We cry; we talk; and incredibly, the funeral is scheduled two days later, just before my return to the UK.

A large crowd attended from the wider family, perhaps a hundred and twenty people. I am surprised how many people came. I give a speech, thanking various family members for looking after her and reminding everybody what a remarkable woman she was. "Michael, Andrew and Maria, thank you for looking after her so well for so long."

I felt guilty for playing such a minor role in her care. I told the crowd, "What matters is not what you say, but what you do." I choke over those last words and excuse myself, but by that time everybody is in tears.

My mother was an extremely clever, articulate, cultured person who gave up a lot of her life to have six children with the man she loved. He died at the age of forty, leaving her to look after all of us, financially secure but with little practical help. She never got over my father's death and had recurrent episodes of depression, shutting herself off from us and providing for us physically but not emotionally. Having no father and a depressed mother was difficult for all of us. Hardly any family or friends came to the house after his death.

We were isolated, and for some of us, it had lasting effects. My relationship with my mother was complex and unsatisfactory. She was a dour woman, unable to show any physical affection towards her children. I have no memory of ever being hugged by her. I think she simply wasn't capable of doing this: she loved us, but not in a warm, demonstrative way, even before my father's death. I have been very different with our children; I am deliberately tactile, and we hug each other most times we meet.

## The way doctors work: The culture of machismo

I have asked a number of people to read and comment on my book, and there is a common theme that my readers have asked me to address. Throughout my career I have worked in a number of difficult environments: there is too much work and lots of stress. I describe a world where the time allotted to work has no limits, where working hard is one of the measures by which one is judged (although of course, in itself working hard doesn't make you a good doctor). I have a huge capacity for working hard, past the point of tiredness, and this has been a useful attribute. However, far more important than this is what you do with the time.

Working from 8:00 am to 6:30 pm without any breaks is not desirable. Eating lunch in five minutes in front of one's computer and not talking to anyone should not be regarded as normal work behaviour. It's unnecessary and uncaring. Why do we allow it to continue? It's not just the NHS: it permeates all of medicine.

When I worked in America, some of my colleagues would arrive at their office at 6:00 in the morning to show that they were working hard. Of course, this isn't a balanced way of living; it means you don't see your family in the morning. This way of working also discriminates against women (and men) who have childcare responsibilities and those who can't deal with this amount of stress.

Some will argue that jobs such as mine are difficult and pressured, and you need to select people who can handle this work environment, but I don't agree. Applicants for medicine know it's hard: we don't need any additional barriers. This harshness is common to other high-performing areas of employment (e.g.

the legal profession), where there is no legal limit to working hours and where prestigious 'Magic Circle' London law firms have hotel facilities in their buildings so employees don't 'need' to go home to eat and sleep (or see their families!).

This total disregard for work-life balance flies in the face of our clear need to preserve our mental health and not prioritise work over personal relationships. Ultimately, the employer will not gain from this—it is not sustainable, and their employees won't be balanced, normal people that function well in the workplace and make good decisions. It also has the undesirable effect of distancing doctors from their patients.

There is considerable resistance to change. Junior doctors have a much better deal than people of my generation, and it's hard not to feel a little jealous. I often hear older doctors speak out against the EU work regulations that mandate adequate time to sleep, lunch breaks, and recovery time from on-call work. ('In my day, we didn't break for lunch. It didn't do me any harm. It toughens doctors up'.) In fact, as doctors espousing these views retire, these attitudes will be replaced with more modern, caring ones.

## On retirement

I knew I would miss the patients and my colleagues. What I don't miss is the constant stress, the feeling of having too many balls in the air, and the exhaustion after a hard day or week. I wanted to stay involved in advising about patient care, remain up to date and have the intellectual stimulation that medicine brings. I take part in two national meetings (MDTs) that provide advice about ALL patients. These meetings each take an hour every fortnight, and I sometimes miss them if I have other, personal commitments.

I am also frequently consulted by email about patients, and I am remaining involved in ALL research, as a senior adviser. I do all this work for nothing; in fact, I have to pay to do it because giving advice requires continued registration with the General Medical Council.

Retirement will change as time passes but at the moment I am doing the right amount of 'work' and I have never been bored. I am giving quite a lot of international talks for Pharma (this work is remunerated) to fulfil one of my retirement goals: to improve the management of ALL worldwide. I have lectured to doctors about ALL from more than sixty countries and the feedback suggests I am on the way to achieving that goal.

# Glossary

| | | |
|---|---|---|
| A&E | – | accident and emergency department |
| ALL | – | acute lymphoblastic leukaemia |
| BMT | – | bone marrow transplantation or blood and marrow transplantation |
| CAR T-cells | – | chimeric antigen receptor T-cells |
| CLL/SLL | – | chronic lymphocytic leukaemia/small lymphocytic lymphoma |
| CML | – | chronic myeloid leukaemia |
| CNS | – | clinical nurse specialist |
| CT scan | – | computerised tomographic scan |
| EMA | – | European Medicines Agency |
| FDA | – | Food and Drug Administration (USA) |
| FRS | – | Fellow of the Royal Society |
| GA | – | general anaesthetic |
| GMC | – | General Medical Council |
| GP | – | general practitioner |
| ICU/ITU | – | intensive care/therapy unit |
| lab | – | research laboratory where PhDs are done |
| MDT | – | multidisciplinary team meeting |
| MGUS | – | monoclonal gammopathy of uncertain significance, a 'pre-myeloma' disease |
| MHRA | – | Medicines and Healthcare products Regulatory Agency (UK) |
| MRI scan | – | magnetic resonance imaging scan, particularly useful for visualising certain parts of the body, that does not involve radiation |

NICE      –   National Institute of Clinical Excellence, a government body in the UK

PPE      –   personal protective equipment

T-cell      –   a type of white blood cell involved in surveillance against viruses and cancer cells. CAR T-cells are genetically modified T-lymphocytes that specifically target certain cancer cells

# Appendix 1
# What Do Leukaemia Patients Want?

Most of all, they want you to care. They want your time and undivided attention. They don't want you to be looking at your phone or answering calls when you talk with them. They may want privacy. They certainly expect you to be completely up-to-date with the literature, and they want (in most cases) to have decisions about their treatment explained to them, in detail, with all the caveats and uncertainties.

Honesty is essential: they want to hear about changes in their status, if they are good, bad or indifferent. When they have a bone marrow or disease assessment, they want the result quickly.

When I have an important discussion with a leukaemia inpatient on the ward, I give them some warning. I always ask them to have somebody else present, and I take along a clinical nurse specialist who knows them. I sit where I can see everybody in the room and make eye contact. I tell them the unadorned truth. My patients trust that I am telling them everything and that I have their interests at the heart of all that I do.

If their leukaemia has a poor prognosis, perhaps with adverse genetic changes, they want to know about it from the beginning and what we are going to do about it: how we can maximise their chances of cure. They don't want their consultant to withhold bad news because of a perception that they won't be able to cope. This attitude is patronising. Most of all, they don't want to hear that their leukaemia was high-risk later in the disease course when things are going badly; that results in them losing trust in you.

From the outset, I promise my patients that I am going to tell them everything and that they don't need to worry that things are worse than I say. I've always done it this way.

# Appendix 2
# The Components of Blood and How We Assess Them

Peripheral blood, obtained from a patient's veins, contains three main types of cells: red cells, white cells and platelets. We use an automated counter to measure the amounts of these cells, and a lot of other parameters of each cell that helps us assess the overall health of each part of the blood system.

Red cells contain haemoglobin, which enables them to carry oxygen to all parts of the body. We measure the haemoglobin level; it should be 120–160 grams per decilitre. Below this range, the person is anaemic. They are likely to feel tired and sometimes short of breath, and they may look pale.

A marrow occupied by leukaemia doesn't make enough red cells: anaemia is a common finding. We also assess red cells by looking at them through a microscope, assessing their shape and measuring their volume. If you are deficient in iron, the red cells are small (microcytic).

White cells are normally at a level of 4–10 x $10^9$ per litre. There are many types, but are broadly divided into granulocytes and lymphocytes. All types of white cells can become cancerous and cause leukaemia. In ALL, the cell that becomes malignant is the primitive lymphocyte (called a lymphoblast). White cell counts are increased in infection or inflammation, and leukaemia.

Leukaemia cells look abnormal and 'primitive'; we see cells in the blood that we normally only see in the bone marrow, the site of the blood cell-making factory. These white cells grow too rapidly, out of control, and don't work normally. They crowd the marrow, leaving insufficient space for normal blood cell manufacture. So, we assess white cells by looking at them under a high-power microscope but also by analysing their chromosomes and various genes that may be mutated.

Platelets are the smallest cells in the blood, responsible for clotting. The platelet count is a sensitive marker of the health of the marrow and is commonly low in patients with leukaemia, meaning that these patients have a tendency to bleed. Sometimes this is in less serious places like the skin or the nasal mucosa, but it can occur in the brain or the lungs. The normal platelet count is 150 to 400 x $10^9$ per litre.

# Appendix 3
# CAR T-Cells

Chimeric antigen receptor T-cells are a new therapy for ALL, lymphoma and myeloma but may be available soon for many other common cancers. They are genetically modified T-cells (a type of white blood cell), taken from the patient, designed to recognise proteins called antigens on the cancer cell surface. They then bind to that antigen and destroy the cell, which releases chemicals called cytokines that attract more CAR T-cells, which then intensifies the destructive process.

This is by far the most powerful therapy we have against leukaemia. A patient can have a marrow totally full of leukaemia cells, receive CAR T-cells and find that all their leukaemia cells can be killed over the next month. Many patients who have had this treatment are well five to ten years later: we believe they are cured, even though nothing else has worked.

T-cells are there to eliminate cancer cells and viruses but sometimes they are overwhelmed. The genetic modifications enhance the ability of the cells to do their job, they enhance the patient's natural immune system. However, there is a complication of the therapy, called cytokine release syndrome (CRS), in which the release of cytokines can make the patient very ill, with low blood pressure and shortness of breath, which may require specific therapies and admission to intensive care for support. CRS is treated with tocilizumab, anakinra and sometimes steroids, all of which inhibit cytokine release or block its action. A small number of adults receiving this therapy have died of this complication.

Moreover, this therapy is very expensive, costing up to half a million pounds per patient and requiring three weeks in a haematology ward, but it sometimes involves the intensive care unit. It does, however, represent the single most important recent change in ALL therapy because we can now cure patients who previously were unresponsive to all treatments. My cancer centre in Bristol was selected to be one of the first six centres in the country to deliver this treatment.

# Appendix 4
# A COVID Fantasy

The piece below, which was read on BBC Radio Bristol Upload in 2020, was written at the height of the epidemic before there was an effective vaccine. Most of this book has been written during the first two years of the pandemic, and it seems important to include this to contextualise the environment we worked in and the fears we all had.

First, a bit about the virus. I have a major interest in viral infection in transplant patients, and I am the infection lead for my cancer centre. From March 2020, I provided expert advice in our cancer centre to minimise the COVID risk to staff and patients. It has been a lot of work. At the time of writing, late in 2020, we know that steroids improve the outcome of COVID pneumonia and there is the promise of a vaccine (although nobody has had it yet, outside of trials).

During the pandemic, many frontline hospital doctors were scared of getting infected with the virus and then developing progressive fever and shortness of breath due to viral pneumonia. Here was a possible sequence of events in early 2020, before we had any therapies or preventative strategies for COVID.

After developing symptoms of the virus, possibly acquired from a patient, I would be at home, quite unwell, spending a lot of time in bed. I became anxious, constantly checking my temperature, hoping it would subside and asking people to listen to my chest with a stethoscope for evidence of pneumonia. Some doctors with COVID bought oxygen saturation meters from Amazon to monitor their progress: these would show a progressive lowering of oxygen levels to the low 90s (95–100% is normal). In the early phases of the pandemic, a radiologist in China posted serial ultrasounds of his lungs on Twitter. It was tense reading: we were all scared his pneumonia would get worse and he would die (his lungs got worse for several days, but then he improved).

In periods when patients were not allowed visitors, I fantasised about being taken to the hospital by my family (or, if I was very ill, by an ambulance), and saying goodbye at the entrance to A&E, knowing that this might be the last time I saw them. I would wait around for hours in a very crowded A&E (among other patients who might be even sicker), but eventually, I would be swabbed, X-rayed and history would be taken. After transferring to one of the COVID wards, I would be seen by a junior doctor who would be worried about looking after me because I am a medical professor (there are both advantages and disadvantages of being ill when you are a doctor yourself). I would have an oxygen mask on, to ease the breathing problems but which would be claustrophobic.

All the staff in the COVID ward would be wearing special, tightly fitting masks, visors, goggles, gloves and gowns: I wouldn't be able to see their faces or know what they were thinking, while also having a clear view of other struggling patients across the respiratory ward. The bleeping oxygen saturation monitor by the bedside would record a decreasing percentage of oxygen and the flow rate of the oxygen would be turned up until it reached 15 L per minute (the maximum). I would be given the steroid dexamethasone and probably the antiviral remdesivir and offered entry onto the national COVID Recovery trial, where I might receive additional therapies. I would desperately want to be randomised to the experimental arm of the trial in the hope of receiving treatments such as antibodies or plasma; when you are extremely ill, you are not interested in helping other people by contributing to the knowledge of the virus and its treatment on the control arm.

All the time, the medics would monitor my respiratory rate, which would slowly increase. Normal is 12–16 breaths times per minute. At the point of deterioration, they would strap on a tight-fitting high-pressure mask (CPAP: continuous positive airways pressure) and the intensive care consultant would come to assess me. This would be awkward because I would know them, but by this time I would be beyond caring.

The consultant would assess me medically, sizing me up as a candidate for intubation, and tell me that they would need to do the intubation pre-emptively before I ran out of breath. Would I have enough respiratory reserve when they removed the tube? I even fantasised about telling the consultant that, although I am sixty-three and a little overweight, I can ride a bike faster than almost any doctor in the ITU (I have ridden from London to Paris).

All the while, my family would be worrying about me, and because the hospital would be so busy, they would have trouble getting through to the ward. I would phone home to tell my wife and children what was happening, that I was moving towards intubation, that I might not wake up again, and that it could be two weeks before the outcome was known. I would do this on the Family WhatsApp group chat, realising that they could see my distress and shortness of breath. The palliative care consultant would come to see me, to ascertain my wishes. This is called 'parallel planning', hoping for the best but preparing for the worst.

She would remind me that I don't have to choose to be intubated, but that if I survived my quality of life might be very impaired. She would explain why they might decide to stop active treatment. Of course, I know the reasons: God knows I have been on the other side often enough, making decisions about patients not doing well in ITU and 'turning them off'. I would ask that my wife be kept informed because I know she will make good decisions while I am sedated; she wouldn't want to keep going if things were hopeless.

Time would be compressed. I would type individual letters to all my immediate family, a brief goodbye email on my laptop, telling them that I love them, that I don't want my death to ruin the rest of their lives, that they should continue to live their lives … and that I might survive! I can barely imagine the effect of receiving such an email.

None of this happened, but it could have. Working as I have done over the last year, I am sure I have had the virus on my hands and probably in my nose, mouth and eyes. I admit I was scared. I even calculated my chance of dying if I got the virus, adjusting for my age and gender: about 1.5–2% of dying, a slow death where you run out of breath. I overcompensated by reading 'everything' about the virus and getting our cancer centre to do sensible things to protect staff and patients from the virus.

# Further Reading

American Cancer Society, *Information about ALL*.
https://www.cancer.org/cancer/acute-lymphocytic-leukemia/about/what-is-all.html.

*The EBMT Handbook*. https://www.ebmt.org/education/ebmt-handbook. For healthcare professionals. Everything you need to know about transplant and CAR T-cells, written by European experts.

Macmillan Cancer Support. *ALL*. https://www.macmillan.org.uk/cancer-information-and-support/leukaemia/acute-lymphoblastic-leukaemia-all.

Sekkeres, M. (2020) *When Blood Breaks Down. Life Lessons from Leukemia*, MIT Press. A well-known American leukaemia physician writes about some of the patients he treated. Quite factual and clinical.

Mukherjee, S. (2010) *The Emperor of all maladies. A biography of cancer*, Scribner. An extraordinary book charting the development of effective cancer treatments, written by a Pulitzer prize winning New York oncologist.

Susan, K. S. (2020) *CAR T-Cell Therapy: What to Expect Before, During and After*, Blood & Marrow Transplant Information Network, https://bmtinfonet.org/.

# Post-Script

**Last days of freedom**

It's Sunday morning: I have a busy week ahead. I am starting my leukaemia treatment on Thursday. On Monday, I will have pre-treatment blood tests, on Tuesday a flexible cystoscopy for my overactive bladder (OAB). (This is a separate problem but it is not a nice test having a scope fed up your penis then the tube is manoeuvred for ten minutes.)

I have difficult veins to cannulate but we have decided to proceed initially without a PICC line. It may not work. The first 2 infusions will last 4 to 6 hours. I will be given high dose intravenous steroids and an antihistamine. There is a high chance of an infusion reaction with fevers and rigors, this will make me unwell and will make the infusion even slower.

The treatment has been expedited and will occur in the teenage and young adult unit (TYA) so that I have some privacy. I don't really want my colleagues walking past and to have to chat to them out of politeness. Nor do I want to sit next to one of my old patients. I do believe I deserve this: it's the least they can do given I have worked there for over a quarter of a century.

I then have infusions on day 8, 15 and 29—a very heavy program. Before the day 29 infusion, I will start venetoclax which is renowned for being almost too effective in killing leukaemia cells. Monitoring and preventing this 'tumour lysis' means lots more blood tests. No blood test is routine for me, it needs the PICC team and that means more waiting and more time. I'm not very good sitting in a chair for 6 hours, waiting to see if I get ill. It will be hard.

**First day of treatment**

The peripheral line went in easily; the PICC team hasn't missed yet. Touch wood, they all know me now. JP, the leader of the team, is a legend in the Oncology Centre.

I walked to the other side of level five to the TYA unit. The male Italian nurse Sev greeted me, he had the antibody in his hand from the fridge. "I've set up the near cubicle, is that ok for you?" He was short, with Italian dark set features and a soft smile. Not at all daunted at looking after a professor of Haematology. Fine with me. The cubical had a protective curtain for privacy, a central reclining chair somewhat similar to a dentist's chair, and a narrow bench behind for visitors. All off white and muted blues and greys but with a window behind. I had brought my laptop, a novel which I didn't feel like reading, lots of drinks and some food. I needed close observation and wouldn't be allowed to leave the cubicle except to go to the toilet.

They did my obs and then went through the most exhausting checking procedure of the drugs, the protocol, my consent form, my pre-assessment tests. Sev gave me my 3 pre-meds (steroid, anti-histamine and paracetamol) and flushed the two intravenous drugs. An hour later, not a minute earlier, the obinatuzumab (a monoclonal antibody directed against B cells) was put up, at a rate of 25mg per hour. I had observations done every 30 minutes but they kept coming by, asking me how I was feeling. I watched the cricket on my laptop, a welcome diversion.

After about 2 hours, I reported feeling a bit 'weird', just strange and a bit weak. They paused the infusion and I felt fine 5 minutes later. The Reiki therapist arrived with her lavender steam, oriental music and light touch of my feet, head and chest. It passed the time and took me 'out of myself'. It was then I had a slight pressure in my lower chest. It wasn't due to the therapist! This lasted 5 minutes. The nurse paused the infusion, called the registrar who came about half an hour later. He examined my chest (which was normal) and said to restart the infusion.

I then developed a fever which rose to 37.7 and a fast heart rate up to 120 per minute. I felt sweaty but not unwell. They paused the infusion again, gave me more pre-meds. We then restarted but I remained a bit hot and was aware of my fast heartbeat. We continued the infusion in spite of the grade 2 infusion reaction. It took in total about 7 hours to get the 100mg in. Sev my assigned nurse, was lovely and seemed to enjoy the fairly busy day, even though I was the only patient.

I wanted to walk home but my wife wouldn't allow me. The line was taken out, I pressed on the vein for 5 minutes, there was no bruising: vein preserved. I spent only half the day in the treatment chair, most of it on the narrow bench with my laptop.

When I got home, I was fine. Day 1 was over. The antibody would be circulating in my blood, marrow and lymph nodes, killing CLL cells. Go for it. Day 2 would be a much higher dose and would be a long day. I knew I would not sleep that night because of all the steroids I had been given. Just pleased to have crossed the day off the list.